a gift for

_____

presented by

_____

"This book paints a picture of every situation I can think of and shows how we can actually pray without ceasing. Trust me, you can not only put your laundry away, you can accomplish all you need to do in a day while praying. Let Tracy paint for you a multitude of prayer visuals as she has painted them for me."

—THELMA WELLS, PRESIDENT, A WOMAN OF GOD MINISTRIES, SPEAKER FOR WOMEN OF FAITH

"Moms, if you want more energy and power in your life, you've come to the right place. Prayer Starters for Busy Moms is the book for you, and Tracy Klehn is the woman to show you how to get started."

—ALLISON GAPPA-BOTTKE, AUTHOR/FOUNDER, GOD ALLOWS U-TURNS

"Too busy to pray? Too busy to read a book on how to pray? Here's the answer for you in a fun-filled book. Here you will find, in brief practical pages, answers and suggestions that will open the gates to God for you!"

—FLORENCE LITTAUER, SPEAKER, AUTHOR OF JOURNEY TO JESUS

TRACY KLEHN

prayer
starters
for busy moms

how to **pray all day**

and **still**

put the **laundry away**

365
creative
ideas

Prayer Starters for Busy Moms
Copyright © 2006 Tracy Klehn

Cover & Interior Design by DeAnna Pierce, Mark Mickel, Brand Navigation, LLC
Photography by Getty Images/Angela Wyant

Published by Bethany House Publishers
11400 Hampshire Avenue South
Bloomington, Minnesota 55438

Bethany House Publishers is a division of
Baker Publishing Group, Grand Rapids, Michigan.

Printed in China

ISBN-13: 978-0-7642-0175-2
ISBN-10: 0-7642-0175-1

Library of Congress Cataloging-in-Publication Data

Klehn, Tracy
  Prayer starters for busy moms : how to pray all day and still put the laundry away.
  / Tracy Klehn
    p. cm.

  Summary: "Whether lumbering over laundry or tripping over toys, busy moms need
help. This book offers practical and inspirational ideas to make their prayer lives
pop!"—Provided by publisher.

  ISBN 0-7642-0175-1 (hardback : alk. paper)

  1. Mothers—Religious life. 2. Prayer—Christianity. I. Title.

BV4529.18.K64 2006

  242'.6431—dc22

                                                              2005023662

to the men *in* my life...

God the Father, Jesus Christ, and the Holy Spirit
This book is my "alabaster jar."

Grandpa, Dad, and Russ
Thank you for loving me.

And to my "littlest man and woman"
Your births ushered me into the presence of the Lord.

acknowledgments

I have been greatly influenced by people who have given God a wholehearted "YES!"

Through their words (whether spoken, written, or sung) and actions I have experienced the power and love of Jesus Christ. For this I am eternally grateful.

I specifically thank...

Dave and Sue White and my family at NorthPark Community Church. You "live it" and inspire me to do the same.

My family and friends for the love, support, and patience that you have extended to me throughout the years.

Marita and Florence Littauer. Through CLASS I have been trained, encouraged, and given opportunities to serve the Lord.

Fern Nichols. Thank you for starting Moms In Touch and thank you for coming alongside this project.

My "Glorieta Angel," Allison Gappa-Bottke. Thank you for opening doors as well as reading, instructing, and cheering me on.

Thelma Wells. I am still overwhelmed by the fact that I have a Woman of Faith that believes in these words. Your speaking ministry has changed me.

Becky Tirabassi. Prayer has indeed "changed my life."

Kyle, Julie, and Bethany House. This opportunity is literally a "dream come true."

Afton Rorvick. Thank you for the grace and truth throughout the editing process. You have "sharpened" this book.

Brennan Manning, Dolley Carlson, Patsy Clairmont, and all of the Women of Faith; Cece Winans, Steven Curtis Chapman, Joyce Meyer, and Father Patrick Martin.

contents

introduction:

"beeping *and* overfloating"

Prayer opens our hearts to God. Our prayers are the means by which our souls, though empty, are filled by God to overflowing.

—JOHN BUNYAN[1]

As I drove the carpool one cold winter's morning, my six-year-old daughter, Grace, announced exuberantly from the backseat: "Jesus loves me, I can feel it!" I smiled to myself and giggled as I responded, "That's so nice, honey. What does it feel like to you?" She pondered this question quietly for a few moments before answering: "Well, my heart is beeping." Her friend added, "And mine is overfloating!"

I have some questions for you:

> *Is your heart "beeping" and "overfloating"?*
> *Do you feel the love that Jesus has for you?*
> *Do you experience his love and his power flowing through*
> *your heart and life in real ways?*
> *Do you know for a fact and never doubt that he does*
> *indeed love you?*

Scripture states in the book of Proverbs: "What a man [woman] desires is unfailing love" (Proverbs 19:22). Has your desire for unfailing love been fulfilled?

If someone had asked me these questions nine years ago, I would have answered them all with a resounding *"No!"* As far back as I can remember, I was intellectually aware of the fact that Jesus loved me, but did I feel it and live out of it? No. But then something took place that changed all of that....

I began to pray.

I began to pray at a very critical time in my life. It was a time when I often felt depleted, isolated, unattractive, and tremendously needy. You can probably guess that I'm describing the early years of motherhood. The years I had hoped would be the happiest and most memorable of my life seemed primarily filled with sleepless nights, endless laundry, spit-up, and dirty diapers.

As I look back on it now, the most illuminating moment and therefore the turning point for me was when an enthusiastic young speaker by the name of Becky Tirabassi informed me, "Prayer is a two-way conversation, one in which you talk to God and then you listen to God speak to you."[2]

This was a totally new concept for me—that God wanted to talk to me, help me, love me through the avenue of

prayer. In years past, I had categorized praying as another thing I wasn't doing well. Prayer seemed to be the perpetual New Year's resolution that I would give up on in February. When I realized that prayer was not about "shoulds" or "oughts" but about a vibrant two-way relationship with the living God, my attitude toward prayer changed completely, and as a result completely transformed my life. I began to look forward to my prayer time with God, and I began to expect and antici-pate that he would have things to tell me. Prayer became an exciting adventure!

Once praying became a regular part of my day, it was as if someone had handed me a lifetime subscription to my favorite magazine, had signed me up for one of those bouquets of flowers each month, or had taken me by the hand and led me to a warm and inviting fire that burned constantly in the next room.

Prayer...

- helped me to experience more power, more peace, and less fear.

- enabled me to be more present with my husband and children.

- invited me to rest in the knowledge that in mothering my children, I was accomplishing something of great purpose and importance to God.

- ushered me into the warmth and light of God's unfailing love.

It was through prayer that I began to feel the love of God in powerful ways. Or, as my daughter and her friend would say, it was through prayer that I found my heart "beeping" and "overfloating."

To this day I continue to feel grateful for the timing God had for me with prayer. Those early years of motherhood were uniquely challenging, and I desperately needed God and his power at that time in my life.

Prayer has had such an impact on me that I actually asked God for over two years to inspire me with a message on the topic of prayer that would encourage others, specifically mothers like you, to enthusiastically join in. The book you are now holding in your hands is the answer to that prayer.

Prayer Starters for Busy Moms will help you "ask," as well as confess, praise, lament, rejoice, weep, wait.... Keep it close to you and let it remind you that there is Someone ready to love, listen, and guide you!

how to use this book

You can use this book in several ways. You can read it from start to finish. You can read one idea for each day of the year. If the bathroom is the only place you seem to get any alone time, you can read this book there in little bits. You can even open the book up on an as-needed basis and put into practice the idea that you come upon that day. The goal of this book is to get you *into relationship with God* and keep you from that place of regulations, rule-following, and self-condemnation that we as mothers can so easily slip into.

Each chapter contains:

1. A brief story related to the theme of the chapter.

2. The first "Prayer Starter," which is a scriptural prayer. One of the blessings of praying scripturally is the knowledge that you are praying God's will. Pray God's Word and remain in God's will.

3. Other simple and practical Prayer Starters: "A full life of prayer contains infinite variety."[3] These Prayer Starters have titles that offer suggestions for when and where you can use this prayer. The titles are meant as a guide. Don't let them keep you from praying whenever you feel like talking to God.

4. A final Prayer Starter, which is a Scripture to meditate on and memorize. As you hide Scripture in your heart, you have more power over the enemy. Did you know that the only offensive weapon in the armor of God is the Sword of the Spirit, which is the Word of God?

5. A short poem, prayer, or song that speaks of the wonder of prayer.

The last chapter of this book offers some practical suggestions for starting and finishing your day with prayer.

Join me on this adventure of prayer. Come and draw near the warm, inviting fire.

1
drawing near *the* fire:
the premise *of* prayer starters *for* busy moms

We pray without ceasing because God loves without ceasing and it is through the ACTION of prayer that this love comes ALIVE and is experienced in flesh and blood. My flesh, God's blood.

It was the second week in September and the second week of school for the kids when I found myself making this journal entry:

It is 8:00 on Thursday morning. I have already...

- gotten up out of bed (at 5:23)

- taken my allergy medicine

- been on a walk

- done lunges and sit-ups, even though I hate them both

- showered (the long tedious one, which means I even shaved my legs)

- woken the kids up

- given out consequences to my daughter (she lost her television privileges for the day)

- confessed to the Lord I was angry and had a bad attitude as I gave out consequences to my daughter

- said a quick "SOS" prayer for patience

- wrote a note to the teacher and put it in my son's backpack

- made lunches and loaded them in backpacks

- made breakfast for the kids and shoved a PowerBar™ in my mouth along with a handful of vitamins

I have also...

- done my daughter's hair

- made my bed

- gotten the car seat out of our car for carpooling

- done the dishes

- looked for Spencer's school uniform shorts and found them shoved in the bottom of his pants drawer

- tumbled them in the dryer to get the wrinkles out

- refolded everything in his pants drawer and his shorts drawers

- started a load of laundry

- hugged and kissed my children good-bye

- settled them in the neighbor's car for carpooling

- made a cup of tea

- and finally sat down!

NO WONDER I'M TIRED!

As a mom, and as a woman in general, doesn't it seem that the only thing that is "without ceasing" in our lives is the demand on our time and energy with the needs of the world, mainly the world in our own home? Yet Scripture tells us:

Rejoice always, pray without ceasing, in everything give thanks; for this is the will of God in Christ Jesus for you.
1 THESSALONIANS 5:16-18 NKJV

Is this some kind of cruel joke? Why would God call us to *do* more? Doesn't he see that we're dying here? Doesn't he see that we're barely holding on, barely getting by? How are we supposed to fit prayer into this life when we can't even fit lunch in most days!?

I believe that kind of thinking represents a huge misunderstanding about prayer, because prayer isn't about *doing* more. It is about *being* in an intimate relationship with the One who loves us the most and is able to meet all of our needs. Prayer is the channel through which the love of God flows into our hearts and *then* out to the world.

When I began preparing this chapter, I asked several faithful people to tell me what motivates them to keep on praying. The answers that I received held a similar theme.

I miss God when we're not together.

I can feel a difference in my life, an intimacy, a connection when I pray. When that's missing, there's loneliness, there's emptiness.

These people missed the connection, the overflowing relationship with God. Through the action of prayer, they were able to experience love and fullness rather than loneliness and depletion. This has been my experience as well.

So where do we start? How do we begin to access this love? That's where this book comes in. I hope that by applying the practical ideas in the chapters ahead, your communication with God will become even more constant and intimate, enabling you to remain in that loved place more consistently. It is in this place of prayer that the power of God is released. According to Ephesians 1:18–19, this power is available for you.

I pray also that the eyes of your heart may be enlightened in order that you may know the hope to which he has called you, the riches of his glorious inheritance in the saints, and his incomparably great power for us who believe. That power is like the working of his mighty strength.

Translated into more contemporary terms, *The Message* puts Ephesians 1:18–20 like this:

I ask...the God of our Master, Jesus Christ...that you can...grasp the immensity of this glorious way of life he has for Christians, oh, the utter extravagance of his work in us who trust him—endless energy, boundless strength! All this energy issues from Christ.

Power, energy, strength...doesn't that sound like what you need as a mother, as a woman, as a child of God?

This first chapter of *Prayer Starters for Busy Moms* is uniquely formatted in that there are only five Prayer Starters. This chapter explains the true starting place on this prayer adventure. Please join me in taking a moment to lay this foundation.

In the introduction I compared prayer to discovering a fire constantly burning in the next room. *Prayer Starters for Busy Moms* is like being given a book of matches. In order to see the fire that a match can create, you must actively open the book, pull out a match, and strike it against the appropriate surface. When you add kindling, paper, and wood to this small flame, a roaring fire results.

So open this little book, pull out one idea, and begin to pray. When you add praise, confession, and the Word of God to this small flame, a blaze is sure to occur. A fire that is bright, beautiful, and powerful. Prayer is the act of drawing near the fire.

And so I ask you...is there a fire in your heart? Is the home of your heart alive with the love of God? Are others drawn to the fire in your heart?

The "prayer of salvation" contained in this chapter is the most important of the Prayer Starters because this is where all of life begins. Jesus is the source of love and of eternal life. He tells us personally in John 10:10: "I have come that they may have life, and have it to the full."

I was once invited to come to the fire by a woman who was not herself the source of the fire, but was one who had stood near to the source and experienced its warmth, power, light, and life. I now extend that same invitation to you. Will you come? Will you draw near? Will you allow the source of the fire—God—to flow through you? Will you receive the power of God into your life?

I truly believe that God is waiting for you to come and be with him. Won't you join him? Let's pray.

God loves me

I acknowledge that God loves me and has good
plans for me.

> *"For I know the plans I have for you,"*
> *declares the LORD, "plans to prosper you*
> *and not to harm you, plans to give you hope*
> *and a future."*
>
> **JEREMIAH 29:11**

the problem *of* sin

I know that the problem is sin and that my sin separates
me from God and brings me spiritual death. This separa-
tion does not allow me to experience the love that God
has for me.

> *For all have sinned and fall short*
> *of the glory of God.*
>
> **ROMANS 3:23**

confess

I openly admit and confess my sin. (Journal
any actions, attitudes, or deeds in which you
have gone your way instead of God's way.)

*If we confess our sins, he is faithful and just
and will forgive us our sins and purify us
from all unrighteousness.*

1 JOHN 1:9

I need Jesus

I see my need for a Savior. I understand that
Jesus Christ paid the penalty for my sin and
that his death and resurrection offer me the gift
of eternal life.

*For the wages of sin is death, but the gift of
God is eternal life in Christ Jesus our Lord.*

ROMANS 6:23

receive *the* fire

I choose to receive Jesus Christ into my heart, knowing
that it takes more than just belief; it takes the action of
receiving. I do this by praying this prayer:

*Jesus, I thank you for dying for my sins past, present,
and future. I need you desperately. I open the door of
my heart and ask you to come in. Make your home in
my heart, set my heart ablaze. Be Lord of my life,
pouring your Holy Spirit into every nook and cranny
until it overflows into the world around me. Amen.*

*Yet to all who received him, to those who believed in
his name, he gave the right to become children of God.*
JOHN 1:12

Congratulations! You have just made the most important deci-
sion of your life, and in doing so you have laid the foundation
for *Prayer Starters for Busy Moms,* a time of intimate, powerful, and exciting communication between you and God.

*O Israel, put your hope in the LORD, for with the LORD
is unfailing love and with him is full redemption.*
PSALM 130:7

32

"drawing near"

A candle burning
The porch light on
A fire popping
I am at home

I nestle down
On a cozy chair
I drink in the scene
I breathe in the air

The Promise reads
He's always here
His presence warm
His Spirit near

And so I come
To release my cares
Unto the Lord
Who hears my prayers

2 prayers *that* start *as* you breathe

*Prayer is exhaling the spirit of man
and inhaling the spirit of God.*

—**EDWIN KEITH**

I set my daughter's fuchsia-colored boom box down as I got ready to listen to a tape by Brennan Manning. I settled down on the chaise and covered up with a blanket, ready to take in the teaching. My husband and children played happily in the front yard, and the rest of the house was quiet. I chose to embrace the moment of tranquility even though the laundry continued to glare at me from the corner of the room.

Brennan spoke passionately about the grace of Jesus Christ, and of how Jesus has taught us to go to God the Father as he himself did, addressing God in the casual and intimate term *Abba,* which in contemporary times translates to *Daddy.*

As I listened to the tape, I heard someone come into the house and walk down the hall. I turned and saw my daughter standing in the doorway. I smiled, she smiled back, and then she turned and scampered down the hall and back outside.

Brennan went on to say,
"The greatest gift any ragamuffin can receive from Jesus is the Abba experience. Jesus says we are to go to God with the unaffected simplicity of a child with his daddy...a youngster of two or three who has been toddling around exploring the mysteries of his father's flashlight, key chain, and assorted coins left on an end table. The little ragamuffin suddenly wearies and staggers back into his mother's arms. Soothed by her affectionate words as she strokes his hair, the little

guy falls asleep, tranquil and quiet. Jesus invites us to become like a little child, to crawl into Abba's arms and let him love on us."[2]

I was contemplating this beautiful analogy when I noticed for the second time that my daughter had walked quietly to my room and again stood in the doorway. We repeated our silent gaze and smile routine and then once again parted ways.

It was the third of my daughter's trips down the hall that reminded me of the tender mercy of my Abba. For on this trip, Grace came across the threshold holding a stuffed pony in one hand and her blanket in the other. As she walked toward me, I lifted my blanket to welcome her, and she climbed up onto my lap without a word. Once she had nestled down, I began stroking her hair, and she gradually drifted off to sleep. I listened to the last part of the tape with tears streaming down my cheeks. In case I had not fully grasped the concept of prayer that Brennan was describing,

God had given me an "object lesson." This was how I was to come to him, in complete trust that I would be loved as I climbed up onto God's lap.

Brennan completed his teaching by explaining that as you breathe, you can be praying every minute of every day. "Abba, I belong to you" is a simple seven-syllable sentence that coincides beautifully with the rhythm of your breath. On the inhale you say, "Abba," and on the exhale you say, "I belong to you."

I began to pray silently in this way, the arms of the chaise cradling my body as I imagined them to be the arms of my Abba. Time seemed to stand still as I experienced peace and security in new ways.

The boom box clicked off, drawing me abruptly from my prayer. As my eyes opened, they came to rest on my daughter's hands. They lay empty and open, the toy having fallen from her grip as she had entered an even deeper state of relaxation and rest, safe within my arms.

scriptural prayer

I love the L<small>ORD</small>, for he heard my voice; he heard my cry for mercy.

Because he turned his ear to me, I will call on him as long as I live.

PSALM 116:1–2

the song

Read the words of this song by Steven Curtis Chapman and pray that this type of an attitude toward prayer would grow in your heart.

"Let Us Pray"
Let us pray, let us pray, everywhere in every way.
Every moment of the day, it is the right time.
For the Father above, He is listening with love.
And He wants to answer us, so let us pray.
Let us pray everywhere in every way.
Every moment of the day, it is the right time.
Let us pray without end and when we finish start again.
Like breathing out and breathing in, let us pray.[3]

STEVEN CURTIS CHAPMAN

first *and* last

This morning when you wake up, lie in bed for a little longer and pray as Brennan Manning instructed: "Abba, I belong to you." This evening as you drift off to sleep, let these be your last words, your last thought, your last prayer.

chore time prayers

As you do the dishes, the laundry, or the vacuuming today, breathe the prayer "Abba, I belong to you." This can turn every moment into a sacred one and help you as you seek to "do all in the name of the Lord Jesus."

COLOSSIANS 3:17 NKJV

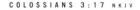

pray when you *are* pooped

Some days you just start out tired, especially if you were forced to share your bed with more than one child the previous night. Other days you may not "hit the wall" until the late afternoon. Whenever you find yourself tired this day, breathe the prayer, "Abba, I belong to you."

pray *it* away

When you find yourself feeling anxious or worried today, breathe this prayer: "Abba, thank you for your peace."

climb *into* his lap

Find a cozy place to sit (preferably a chair that has arms), close your eyes, and rest your hands on your lap, palms up, and breathe the prayer "Abba, I belong to you" for about five minutes. Imagine that the place you are resting is the lap of God the Father.

carpool *and* waiting room serenity

As you drive in the car today, breathe, "Abba, I belong to you." (This is especially helpful when you are stuck in traffic!) When you find yourself waiting in a line (at the bank, at the post office, at the grocery store) breathe this prayer.

the Jesus prayer

Try the most famous of the breath prayers, the "Jesus Prayer," based on Luke 18:13: "'God, have mercy on me, a sinner.'"

In the book The Way of a Pilgrim, *a Russian peasant tells how he traveled from village to village and monastery to monastery trying to find someone to teach him how to pray unceasingly (1 Thessalonians 5:17). Finally, he finds a monk who teaches him the Jesus Prayer by reading to him the following words of St. Symeon the New Theologian: "Sit down alone and in silence. Lower your head, shut your eyes, breathe out gently and imagine yourself looking into your own heart. Carry your mind, i.e., your thoughts, from your head to your heart. As you breathe out say: 'Lord Jesus, have mercy on me.' Say it moving your lips gently, or say it in your mind. Try to put all other thoughts aside. Be calm, be patient and repeat the process very frequently."*

ANTHONY M. CONIARIS[4]

breathe *the* Word

Choose one of your favorite verses and make it your breath prayer. It is helpful if it is short (preferably seven to eight syllables). Here are some examples:

> *Do not be afraid, for I am with you.* ISAIAH 43:5
>
> *It is God who arms me with strength.* PSALM 18:32
>
> *Teach me your way, O LORD.* PSALM 27:11

fidgety *and* distracted

When you are having a difficult time focusing, breathe a prayer. My daughter was sitting next to me in church, and even after several "reminders" was not sitting still. As a result I was distracted and quickly becoming annoyed. It struck me that even when I place myself in the "best possible" environment for a felt experience of God's presence, I am easily distracted mentally and emotionally. In retrospect, this would have been the ideal time to do my breath prayers, whether "Abba, I belong to you" or a short, meaningful Scripture.

alternative
relaxation prayer

When you are stretching or you are in the relaxation portion of your exercise class, pray, "My soul finds rest in you alone" (based on Psalm 62:1) as you focus on your breathing.

breathing his name

Do you realize that your very breath can be powerful? Not only because of the amazing physiological occurrences that happen in your body through the oxygen transport system, but if on your breath, you utter the name of Jesus, you can trust that you are praying in a powerful way. Whisper the name *Jesus* today as often as you can. When you do not know what else to pray, just saying *Jesus* is enough.

The name of the LORD is a strong tower; the
righteous runs into it and is safe.
PROVERBS 18:10 NASB

passionate prayer

After seeing the powerful movie *The Passion of the Christ,* I was captivated by the Aramaic pronunciation of Jesus' name. It is *Yeshua.* Say that out loud. Doesn't it just flow from your tongue? Let the name *Yeshua* be your prayer today. As you fall asleep, say *Yeshua* over and over again.

his name

In *The Peace and Power of Knowing God's Name,* Kay Arthur teaches: "In biblical times, a name represented a person's character. God's name represents His attributes, His nature. His name is a statement of who He is. And He has many names! Each reveals something of His power and love and purposes toward you."[5]

> *Let him who walks in the dark,*
> *who has no light,*
> *trust in the name of the LORD*
> *and rely on his God.*
> **ISAIAH 50:10**

elohim: *the* creator

When you are questioning who is in charge or feeling worthless, invaluable, or insecure, utter this name of the Lord. Speak it also when you are admiring the beauty of God's creation.

el elyon: *the* God most high

When you know there are idols in your life and you need repentance and deliverance from them, utter this name of Jesus. Speak it also when your problems feel insurmountable or when you feel the need or desire to enter into worship.

el roi: *the* God who sees

When you are feeling betrayed, missed, invisible, or unappreciated, utter this name of the Lord. Speak it also when you are caught up in the wonder of the ways the Lord communicates to you specifically and personally.

el shaddai: *the* all-sufficient one

When you feel fearful, needy, desperate, controlling, or angry, or when you need nurturing and mothering, utter this name of the Lord. Speak it also when you feel grateful for the ways God continues to provide for all of your needs. (See Isaiah 49:15-16.)

adonai: *the* Lord

When you want control, when you are feeling hurt and afraid, or when you want to surrender your life or a circumstance in your life to God, utter this name of the Lord. Speak it also when you feel grateful for God's wisdom and his way.

jehovah: *the* self-existent one

When you are questioning your faith or seeking to know more, or when you are struggling with unbelief, doubt, or fear, utter this name of the Lord. Speak it also when God has transformed your unbelief and increased your faith.

jehovah-jireh: *the* Lord will provide

When you are feeling hungry, thirsty, wanting, jealous, envious, when you are feeling fearful about finances or external circumstances, or when you are feeling emotionally needy, utter this name of the Lord. Speak it also when you feel grateful for the miracles, big and small, in your life.

jehovah-rapha:
the Lord who heals

When you are feeling sick or you are concerned about someone who is sick, when you are feeling emotionally or spiritually wounded, or when you are feeling bitter, utter this name of the Lord. Speak it also when you have been healed, delivered, and set free in any of these areas.

jehovah-nissi:
the Lord my banner

When you are feeling tired from the battle and you need renewed strength, when you feel that you are being attacked (spiritual warfare, your flesh), or when you are in need of deliverance from sin and want to experience victory, utter this name of the Lord. Speak it also when you experience victory after a battle has been won.

jehovah-mekoddishkem: *the* Lord who sanctifies you

When you are feeling bad, shame, or guilt, when you are struggling with sin or feeling despair, or when you want someone else to change or you are affected by the sin of others, utter this name of the Lord. Speak it also when you feel grateful about seeing changes in your life or in the lives of those around you.

jehovah-shalom: *the* Lord is peace

When you are feeling frantic, scattered, weary, conflicted, angry, or worried, or when you are being battered by the storms of life, utter this name of the Lord. Speak it also when God has "calmed your storm" and enabled you to experience his peace.

jehovah-sabaoth:
the Lord *of* hosts

When you are feeling desperate and overwhelmed, when you have turned for help everywhere else and come up empty-handed, or when you are in the thick of the battle, utter this name of the Lord. Speak it also when you become aware that God is fighting the battle for you or has indeed delivered you.

jehovah-raah:
the Lord my shepherd

When you need guidance and direction, when you feel lost, hopeless, despairing, or afraid, or when you need rest, utter this name of the Lord. Speak it also when God has brought you to a place of rest and rejuvenation.

jehovah-tsidkenu: *the* Lord our righteousness

When you crave respect and self-confidence, utter this name of the Lord. Speak it also when you become aware of the amazing gift Christ gave you when he died on the Cross, giving you his righteousness in exchange for your sin.

jehovah-shammah:
the Lord *is* there

When you feel alone, abandoned, afraid, or
hopeless, utter this name of the Lord. Speak it
also when you sense the Lord's presence in
very real ways or when he reveals to you that he
was with you at a difficult time in the past.

a verse *to*
meditate upon

> *Our help is in the name of the LORD,*
> *the Maker of heaven and earth.*
>
> **PSALM 124:8**

"chaos prayer"

Lord, in the chaos of the morning routine, may I find myself clear in you, your love, joy, peace, and patience.

When everything is screaming urgently for my attention, may my ear be attuned to your "still, small voice."

When my body is going at a frantic pace, may you keep my spirit in tune with the rhythmic beat of your heart of love and my soul refreshed with your wonderful breath of life.

When I let go of my children day by day, may you hold on tighter and tighter to this child of yours.

Thank you, Abba; I love you, and I desperately need you.

3

prayers *that* start right before *your* eyes

> *We need to inwardly aim our hearts and prayers straight at God's heart, because he is always aiming his love straight at ours.*

A few years into my prayer journey, I teamed up with one of my girlfriends to do a talk on the subject of friendship. In our presentation, we shared an idea from Dolley Carlson's book *Gifts From the Heart*.[1] The idea was to do a mug exchange, and in doing so, commit to pray for the friend with whom you had exchanged a mug. From that moment on, whenever you would see the mug, drink from

the mug, or wash the mug, you would lift up your friend in prayer. My girlfriend and I loved this idea, so we bought cute mugs for each other and made this commitment to pray. Little did we know, shortly thereafter we would go through some very difficult times in our relationship.

During those difficult times, there were many days that I found myself in tears, many days that I found myself bitter, and many days that I found myself wanting to flee the friend-ship entirely. My feelings were not pretty nor did my desires feel very "spiritual."

Yet it was during these times, as I unloaded the dishwasher, that I held a certain mug in my hand. As I felt the weight of the mug in my hand, and as I admired the fruit pattern on it, the Lord reminded me of the commitment I had made to my friend. He also reminded me of the verse in Matthew 5:44: "Love your enemies and pray for those who persecute you." It was natural and easy for me to pray for the people in my

life whom I had warm feelings toward, yet I was not called to love based solely on my feelings.

As I placed that mug on the shelf, I uttered a prayer of blessing over my friend, and while my true desire was to push that mug to the back of the shelf (as I desired to push the pain to the back of my mind), the Lord had me place that mug front and center so that I could pray each day as I opened that cupboard.

I am thankful for this symbol, this visual Prayer Starter. Without it, I cannot honestly say that I would have prayed for my friend very often.

scriptural prayer

Lord, give me the eyes to see as you do so that I can pray in the Spirit on all occasions with all kinds of prayers and requests, with this in mind, that I would always keep on praying for all the saints. (Based on Ephesians 6:18)

be what I see

Prayerfully sing the words to this Irish hymn (translated into English by Mary E. Byrne).

"Be Thou My Vision"
*Be Thou my Vision,
O Lord of my heart;
Naught be all else to me,
save that Thou art.
Thou my best Thought,
by day or by night,
Waking or sleeping,
Thy presence my light.*

love them *with* prayer

Choose a visual symbol that would be a reminder for you to pray for someone that you find challenging to love. It could be a picture, a gift, a handwritten note. Each time you see the symbol, ask the Lord to bless that individual, and ask the Lord to continue to grow in your heart the love that he has for that person.

real live fruit

But the fruit of the Spirit is love, joy, peace, patience, kindness, goodness, faithfulness, gentleness and self-control.

GALATIANS 5:22-23

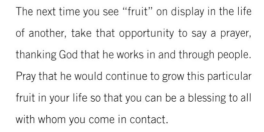

The next time you see "fruit" on display in the life of another, take that opportunity to say a prayer, thanking God that he works in and through people. Pray that he would continue to grow this particular fruit in your life so that you can be a blessing to all with whom you come in contact.

sensing sorrow

Today when you see a person in emotional pain (maybe a friend crying), pray that the Lord would help that person to experience God's peace. You can also pray for the Lord to show you if there is any way that he is calling you to be a comfort to this individual (sending a card, baking some cookies, offering to take care of children).

hand *in* heart

I have a bracelet that was given to me by a new friend. It has a pretty silver hand with a heart cut out in the center of it. She told me that she has the same one. She gave me the gift of her prayers when she gave me this bracelet. Is there a piece of jewelry someone special has given you? Pray for that person when you wear it or even when you see it in your jewelry box.

rocks *and* stones

Our church is in escrow, and many of the people in our congregation have gone to the land and taken a stone or rock to keep on a counter or in their car. This is a visual reminder for them to pray for the continued establishment of the church. Are you in escrow? Looking for a new home? This is a great way to keep that need in view. Find a rock or stone and place it in a highly visible location.

saying grace

Each time you sit down to eat a meal, say a prayer or have your children say a prayer before eating. I grew up saying, "God is great, God is good, let us thank him for our food. Amen." Did you have a prayer that you said growing up? Teach it to your children and tell them the story behind it, or any other funny stories you can remember about praying as a kid. Let your kids make up their own "grace" and then take turns "saying grace."

honor God *with* eating

As you eat, pray that you would honor God by eating only until you are physically full, trusting that he will meet your other emotional and spiritual needs. " 'Everything is permissible for me' —but not everything is beneficial. 'Everything is permissible for me'—but I will not be mastered by anything" (1 Corinthians 6:12).

calendar concerns

Keep a daily tear-off calendar near the kitchen sink. (That's the place I find myself most often during the day!) As you become aware of specific intercession needs (safety for travel, job interviews, surgeries), place the person's name on the appropriate date along with the need. When you get to that date, you will be reminded to lift up those individuals and their concerns in prayer.

cash *and* carried

As you shop this week, thank the Lord for his provision. Each time you pull out your wallet, lift up a brief prayer of thanksgiving to the One who takes care of all your needs.

And my God will meet all your needs according to his glorious riches in Christ Jesus.
PHILIPPIANS 4:19

bookmark prayers

Slip a card from a friend into a book that you are reading (or your journal), and every time you open the book say a prayer for that friend. It is always a special treat when a letter or card falls from a book that you haven't opened in a while and serves as a tangible reminder of a loved one and a helpful reminder to cover that person in prayer.

peace *in the* wilderness

Place a photograph of someone who is going through a difficult season in a place where you will see it regularly. Each time you see the photograph, pray that the person would experience the peace and presence of the Lord that very moment.

red-light prayers

Pray for the person in the car next to you at the stoplight. Pray that he or she would be blessed today and would realize that those blessings are coming from the Lord and that he or she will in turn worship him.

gym prayers

Pray while you are on the exercise bike or treadmill. Pray that the Lord would help you honor him by taking care of your health. If the television is on, allow those images (of war, abducted children, violence) to remind you to pray for the people in those situations.

bedtime blessings

As you rock your little one to sleep, whisper your prayers for him or her. Pray your hopes and dreams for this little person. Pray for future friendships and for a future spouse. When you tuck your older kids in tonight, lay your hands on them and ask the Lord to bless them and continue to grow them into men and women who have a passion for Jesus Christ and a desire to serve him wholeheartedly with all their gifts and talents.

remember *the* miracles

Keep pictures or images in prominent locations in your home of moments I like to call "sacred snapshots." These are times that the Lord has revealed himself to you in very real ways. Some examples might include pictures of your children being born, a picture of a relationship that was restored, a picture of a friend or family member that was healed of a life-threatening illness. The point is to keep them in front of you. We are a forgetful people and can easily be like the Israelites wandering in the desert, grumbling and complaining and forgetting the miracles the Lord has already performed before our very eyes.

Thank you, Lord, for the miracles in my life. The everyday wonders as well as the astounding acts. You are faithful, and I choose to trust you again this day. Amen.

see *the* vision

What is the Lord doing in your life? What is your calling? How has he gifted you? If you are not sure how to answer these questions, begin a vision file. Start tearing out images, words, and sentences from magazines that appeal to you and place them in a file or even a bag. When your file thickens, get out a piece of poster board, scissors, and a glue stick and have fun making a collage. Hang your "vision" where you are sure to see it several times a day, and remember to ask God for his direction.

Where there is no vision...the people perish.
PROVERBS 29:18 AMP

pastor prayers

As your pastor approaches the pulpit to speak this Sunday, pray that the Holy Spirit would pour out his power upon the teaching time. Pray that the Spirit would guide your pastor's words and that the Spirit would also work in the hearts of all those in the congregation.

walk *and* pray

In the book *Prayer Walk*[2] by Janet Holm
McHenry, the author describes how while walk-
ing and praying one morning she saw a young
man hand his young daughter over to a day-
care worker, and she knew God was calling her
to pray for everything she saw along her path as
she walked. Like Janet did, ask God to open
your eyes as you walk today and pray for whatever needs he shows you.

flashing lights

When you see an ambulance or fire vehicle or police car
go by, pray for protection and peace and healing for those
involved in the accident/incident as well as safety and
wisdom for the workers who are going to help. A girlfriend
recently told me that when she was a teenager she wit-
nessed her aunt verbally pray for strangers in a passing
ambulance. That prayer had a profound effect on my
friend: "I was in awe and admiration." Now as an adult
she prays out loud every time she hears sirens blaring.

bulletin board prayers

Place a bulletin board near your kitchen table
and put up pictures of friends and family in
your life. (Use the photos you get from
Christmas cards!) Pray for these people before,
after, or during your meal times.[3]

posted prayers

If you come upon a prayer that touches your
heart, write it out on pretty paper and hang it in
your kitchen next to the coffeepot or teakettle.
In the morning as you wait for your coffee to
drip or your tea to steep, pray this prayer. If
there is not a place to hang it, tape it
to the inside of the mug cupboard. You can find my
"posted prayer" at the
end of this chapter.

sleeping baby

During one of our prayer meetings at school, I held a friend's restless infant. As we continued to pray, she fell fast asleep in my arms, visually reminding me that we are all invited to enter God's rest. The next time you see a baby resting peacefully, pray that you would learn how to enter into the Lord's rest in that same way.

> *"Come to me, all you who are weary and burdened, and I will give you rest."*
> MATTHEW 11:28

crying baby

When you see a child in tears, pray for peace and healing for him or her. Pray for discernment for the parents so that they might know what is bothering the child. Pray that the Lord would arm these parents with his strength, patience, and endurance for this moment and moments in the future.

wild child

Have you ever been at the mall and seen a kid pitching a fit and rolling around in the aisles? Has that been your child (although you pretend you don't know your child in that moment)? Does one of your girlfriends struggle with a strong-willed child? The next time you see this child, pray. Pray for a spirit of self-control to grow in him or her. Pray for wisdom for the parents and for peace for the family. If the parents do not know the Lord, pray that they would come to know him, love him, and worship him.

neighborhood prayers

As you drive around town, pray for the Lord's protection over the different neighborhoods. Is there a particularly rough part of town? As you drive by it or perhaps even reside in it, call out to God for a turning from sin, a lifting of oppression and evil, and for deliverance that would ultimately glorify God.

"purple mountain majesties"

When you see God's "majesty," praise the Lord verbally. For example, if you are driving in the car and see the sky in a flood of colorful clouds, point it out to your children and then say aloud, "Thank you, Lord, for this beautiful world you created. You are awesome!"

"deck *the* halls"

Do an ornament exchange with a girlfriend this year. From now on, when you decorate your tree, pray blessings over this friend's holiday season. You can also do this with ornaments for your children. (As you hang the "Baby's First Christmas" ornament, take a moment to pray for your little one.)

artful reminders

Keep art and pictures in your home that remind you of your Maker. I have a painting by Morgan Weistling hanging in our bedroom. It is a portrait of a young girl clinging to Jesus, her head buried in his chest. I want the first image that I see when I arise to be a reminder that I am held by my Lord, and no matter how difficult the day has been, I want to always be reminded of the One who holds me as I fall to sleep at night.

a verse to meditate upon

Taste and see that the Lord is good.
PSALM 34:8

"a morning prayer"

Jesus, fill this place
This home
This heart
These hands
This face

I long to walk in Your glory
Your strength
Your peace
Your space

Teach me
Show me
Love me
Hold me

My King
My Love
My Savior
My Grace

prayers *that* start *with* praise

When I attended my first Christian conference, I was intrigued by the worship team that led us in praise music. They sang their songs of praise with such freedom and abandon that I experienced a longing to participate with them. Unfortunately, I was all too aware of how others perceived me, and this kept me locked in a prison of people-pleasing and pride.

Eventually, praise and worship unlocked the doors to this prison and freed me to experience blessing upon blessing. I started small, joining in the singing at church and even clapping my hands along with the congregation during the upbeat songs. In the weeks and months that followed, I felt myself becoming less aware of those around me and more aware of the object of my adoration. As I truly began to praise God because he was worthy of my praise, the by-product was that I became less self-centered and self-conscious.

As I would proclaim through songs of praise the awesome attributes of my King, my inward gaze turned "right-side up." Joy began to well up inside of me and pour out of me in the form of lifted hands, closed eyes, and dancing feet. I began to play praise music regularly in my home and in my car. While the simple act of listening to praise music could

have been construed as simply a "pleasant experience," it became for me a way to lift my heart to God in prayers of praise. My daily circumstances became less consuming as my eyes turned to the Lord Most High who in his Sovereignty is able to accomplish "exceedingly abundantly above all that we ask or think" (Ephesians 3:20 NKJV).

Years later at another conference, I stood in the front row, hands held high in worshipful abandon, loving my Lord and Savior Jesus Christ, aware of his love and knowing that because of him everything was going to be okay, no matter what happened.

Lord, my prayer is that your praise will always be on my lips and that my soul will boast in you alone forever and ever. (Based on Psalm 34:1–2)

make *it* my story

When we praise God, he reminds us that we are part of a bigger story, "his story."[2] Sing this hymn and remember your story. Let the refrain become true of you. Thank God for his gift of salvation.

"Blessed Assurance"[3]

Blessed assurance, Jesus is mine!
O what a foretaste of glory divine!
Heir of salvation, purchase of God,
Born of His Spirit, washed in His blood.

This is my story, this is my song,
Praising my Savior, all the day long;
This is my story, this is my song,
Praising my Savior, all the day long.

fill your home

Turn on some praise music or hymns today and sing along. When your heart's desire is to worship Jesus, singing praise can turn the "daily grind" (chores, work, studying, etc.) into an act of prayer, and it can make the ordinary (even taking a bath) an opportunity for a sacred moment.

"pulled out"

As I participated in a lively Bible study discussion group, I was struck by the beauty and truth of what one of the women said.[4] She said, "His glory should pull the praise out of you." Ask God today to show you his glory that you might praise him.

go shopping

Ask some Christian friends and family members who have a grasp of your taste in music if they have any "praise" recommendations for you. Many of the Christian music stores let you listen to demos of CDs before you purchase them. Take a trip today to find a new favorite. Pray that the Lord would guide you to the artist and the songs that would minister to your soul.

give *the* gift *of* praise

Music has a way of touching the deepest parts of the heart, even when it feels hardened or hurting. Has the Lord placed someone on your heart lately? Is there a song that comes to your mind that would minister to that person? Pray the words of that song for your friend and buy her a copy of the music.

get with *the* program

The atmosphere in my car is not always a pleasant one, especially in the morning, when I have been trying to get everybody out the door and to school. It is amazing the transformation that can occur when the car fills with the sound of praise. Program the radio in your car to the Christian stations so that praise is as close as your fingertips. Pray for God's peace to fill your car.

living *in* praise

In Cece Winans' book *Throne Room*,[5] she speaks highly of her father and how he taught her so much about praise and worship. She writes, "He always said that God inhabits the praises of his people (see Psalm 22:3). So I always knew that God wasn't very far away from my dad!" I don't know about you, but one of my regular prayers is "Help me know that you are with me, Lord." As you praise God, revel in the knowledge that he is with you.

multitask

Choose to praise God as you move your body!
Get out your iPod™ and go for a "praise walk."
You can also put some music on in the house
and dance around, praising him (let the kids join
in too!), if you prefer. If you don't have access to
a headset or music, walk anyway and sing the
songs that come to your mind, or even make up
a new song! Let God hear your gratitude.

sing louder *than*
your circumstances

My husband sat next to my ear and hummed sweetly to me
during the birth of our first child. After being induced and
laboring for hours, I ended up in surgery with a C-section.
I told my husband afterward that I thought it was so loving
of him to hum "Amazing Grace" in my ear. His song had
filled me with peace. A few days later he confessed that
the only reason he was singing was so that he wouldn't
have to hear the "surgery noises"! So go ahead today and
sing praises to God. You may just drown out your difficult
circumstances and bless others in the process.

pillow talk

If you wake up with a song on your mind or in your heart,
take note of it. Write it down and meditate on those words.
Find the song and play it if you can. Sing it out loud, and
ask the Lord what he is trying to communicate to you
through this song.

*By day the LORD directs his love, at night his song is with
me—a prayer to the God of my life.*

PSALM 42:8

ask *and* receive

Ask the Lord to speak to you tonight as you
sleep. Ask him to fill your mind and heart with
praise and worship.

*"Ask and it will be given to
you.... If you then, though you
are evil, know how to give good
gifts to your children, how much
more will your Father in heaven
give the Holy Spirit to those who
ask him!"*

LUKE 11:9,13

a posture of boldness

Pray for some "Holy Spirit boldness" this week at church. When you feel compelled to lift your hands, move your feet, or let the tears flow, go for it! Keep in mind that new things can feel uncomfortable, which doesn't make them "wrong," just different. I am reminded of a time when one of my girlfriends began to see a chiropractor. She told me that her posture felt weird because she was used to being out of alignment; however, she knew intellectually that she was on the path to healing and so she continued the treatment. This new posture of praise may just bring healing to you.

praise requests

This morning ask the kids what Christian song they would like to start the day with. (You may need to have them take turns so a "holy war" doesn't break out.) Put that music on while you make breakfast or drive to school, and join with your kids in singing praises and prayers to the Lord. I have been unexpectedly blessed by doing this; my children have often asked for a song the Lord wanted me to hear.

set free *and* singing

Has the Lord done amazing things in your life? Has he rescued you from areas of bondage (addictions, depression, marital struggles)? Take a minute to think about what your life was like before Jesus. Now think about what your life is currently like with Jesus. Take a minute to verbally praise God. Now pray for an opportunity to tell someone what Jesus has done in your life.

He rescued them from the grave. Let them give thanks to the LORD for his unfailing love and his wonderful deeds for men. Let them sacrifice thank offerings and tell of his works with songs of joy.

PSALM 107:20–22

sing them *to* sleep

Ask your child what praise song he/she would like you to sing before bed or naptime. My girlfriend has a bedtime ritual with her children that includes prayers and a praise song for each child—their choice. My kids love sleeping over at their "auntie's," and I can't help but think that this is one of the things they are drawn to in her home. She would be the first to admit that she doesn't have a great singing voice, but to her children the sweet sound of praise helps them drift off to sleep. Let your voice, good or bad, lead your children in praising God at the end of the day.

quiet them *with* praise

If you or your children are anxious or are having a difficult time sleeping, try listening to an instrumental or a
more subdued set of praise music. Let the gentle music
lead you and your children to thanking God for his love.

He will quiet you with his love,
he will rejoice over you with singing.
ZEPHANIAH 3:17

listen *to* your children

The more you praise, the more you will hear your children
humming or singing songs throughout the day. Really listen
to what they are singing. Sometimes it is cute, sometimes
funny, and other times it is profound and meant just for
you. On the night of the presidential election one year,
when anxieties were running high and the votes had not
yet been counted, I heard my daughter singing from the
shower the familiar and comforting words of the hymn
"This Is My Father's World." What a wonderful "Holy
Spirit" reminder this was for me of the sovereignty of God.
Let your children's praise become your praise.

blessings *and* benefits

When you sing praise songs, you may also be memorizing Scripture, because many song lyrics come straight from God's Holy Word. You are filling your heart and mind (not to mention your children's hearts and minds) with the "Sword of the Spirit." A great investment of time and money, in my opinion! Find a song today with words from Scripture. As you sing it, make it your prayer for the day.

growing joy

While driving in Los Angeles, I passed a church that had written on its marquee: "Joy thrives in the soil of praise." I have discovered that when I choose to praise God despite my circumstances, joy really does begin to rise within me. So today when you find yourself in need of a little more joy in your life, choose to pray prayers of praise.

offering praise

Do you play a musical instrument? Offer up your time playing music as a prayer to Jesus today. Get some sheet music of hymns or contemporary Christian music and consider this music your "prayer offering." Do you dance? Offer that as your "prayer offering" today.

alphabet praise

Engage your children in an activity in which you try to come up with attributes and characteristics and names of God in the order of the alphabet. For example: He is Awesome, Beautiful, Counselor.... This is an especially great activity to do when you need to keep little ones occupied on long car rides or plane rides, or when you are waiting at the doctor's office.

praise god *in* prose

In those moments when you are overwhelmed by God's presence and overflowing with praise, take up a pen and write, or open your mouth and speak. In other words, give God back praise for what he has given you.

portable praise

When you know that you will be going on a stressful trip (work or family), bring a portable CD player or iPod™ with you. Steal away from your circumstances and take a "praise walk" with your music or find a quiet place to sit and listen. Let the music bring you back to God and remind you that he is the One in control. Let God, through the music, deliver you from the place of fear and anxiety.

deliverance

Do you need deliverance? Do you feel as if you are sinking? Psalm 32:7 says, "You [God] will protect me from trouble and surround me with songs of deliverance." What songs has the Lord placed on your mind and heart? If you are not aware of any, stop right now, ask, listen, and wait. Do any songs come to mind? If one does, it may very well be your "song of deliverance." Do more than just listen to it though. Pray it, sing it, and live it, believing the truth found in Psalm 32.

serene setting

When you open your home to a play group or to company, put on some quiet praise music. Think of this as creating an environment where the Holy Spirit has an opportunity to minister to the souls of your loved ones or friends. Ask God to speak to you and your guests through this music. This is a beautiful and non-intimidating way to pour "the fragrance of the Lord" on people in your life who may not know the Lord. I opened my home to a group of women a few summers ago for a book study, and I played the same instrumental CD of hymns each time we met. The ladies consistently commented on how comfortable they felt in my home. I knew it was because they were being wrapped in the Spirit.

heavenly chorus

In Revelation 4:6–9 we read about heavenly creatures that "day and night" never stop saying, "Holy, holy, holy is the Lord God Almighty, who was, and is, and is to come." Isn't it awesome to think that praise is always pouring forth in the heavens? God is deserving of our praise, so join the heavenly chorus by repeating this sacred refrain from Revelation as often as you think of it today.

commit

I will sing to the LORD all my life; I will sing praise to my God as long as I live. May my meditation be pleasing to him, as I rejoice in the LORD.

PSALM 104:33-34

"All my life." Wow, that's a long time to sing. This phrase also implies that it's not just on the days I "feel" like singing that I should sing. This psalmist made a pretty bold commitment. Are you ready to do the same? Consider making a commitment today, or reaffirming the commitment that you may have already made to praise God "all your life." He is worthy of our praise.

visualize peace

Once our home became a place where praise music flowed in a constant stream, I became attached to the work of Cece Winans. At a conference I had the opportunity to have a front-row worship experience as Cece led the women in song. As I stood there singing praises, I thought to myself, *Cece's face worshiping the Lord is a picture of peace—peace that dispels fear and communicates "Because of Jesus, everything is going to be okay."* I experienced that peace through praise and worship that day. I now call it "Cece-peace," and I experience it regularly, whether I am standing in a packed conference center or on my knees in my bedroom. Observe those around you worshiping the Lord and pray that you would be able to enter into that worship experience as well.

a verse *to* meditate upon

Praise the LORD, O my soul; all my inmost being, praise his holy name. Praise the LORD, O my soul, and forget not all his benefits— who forgives all your sins and heals all your diseases, who redeems your life from the pit and crowns you with love and compassion, who satisfies your desires with good things so that your youth is renewed like the eagle's.

PSALM 103:1-5

"speaking *the* word"

You are my strength
And You are my song
As I sing praises to You
My heart is made strong

So I stand and rejoice
In this day You have made
I lift hand and voice
In unending praise

When I feel low
Or sad and depressed
I will trust in Your Word
And surely be blessed

5 prayers *that* start *on* the page

Scripture brought me to the gate of paradise, and the mind stood in wonder as it entered.

—EPHREM THE SYRIAN [1]

I grew up going to church, but I did not grow up going to God's Word. I grew up praying to God, but believing that he was preoccupied with more important things (like ruling the universe) than speaking to me directly. That is why it was such a new concept for me that God wanted to communicate with me, and that the primary way in which he would do so was through the Bible.

I learned that God not only loved me but that he also cared about every detail of my life. (See Psalm 139.) He wanted to have a relationship with me, one in which we spent time together and communicated with each other. I learned that by opening the Word and asking the Holy Spirit to open my eyes to understand, I would have the opportunity to hear God's side of the conversation.

This new understanding caused me to go to the Word of God with expectation, trusting that God had something personal and powerful to communicate to me. I began to anticipate that he would have answers to whatever concerned me that day, that month, that season.

Habakkuk 2:1 states, "I will stand at my watch and station myself on the ramparts; I will look to see what he will say to me." When my state of mind shifted from reading the Bible as a "should" to reading the Bible with expectation, every-thing changed. My attitude became one of "Why would I

miss a day in the Word? I might not hear or see what God is telling me!" The "ramparts" became for me my quiet-time chair, and while I might have been physically sitting, I was "standing" in my spirit, expecting the living Lord to speak a personal word to me.

While writing my prayers down may have given me a place to *put* all of the feelings and concerns that were muddled in my heart, going to God's Word *gave me back* what I needed.

scriptural prayer

Lord, I pray that you would "Open my eyes that I may see wonderful things in your law."

BASED ON PSALM 119:18

choose your weapon

I asked my daughter to go get her Bible so that we could finish her homework. Her response was "Okay, but it might be another religion!" I laughed, understanding that she had meant to say "translation." It is important to find the *translation* of the Bible that works for you. Pray that the Lord would help you find it.

easy access

Speaker and author Patsy Clairmont mentioned recently[2] that when her kids were small, she used to keep Bibles *everywhere* she might find herself sitting for a few moments during the day or night. Stock up the "rest stops" in your life (kitchen counter, coffee table, bedside table, bathroom, car) with Bibles. When you have a minute to sit down, pray that the Holy Spirit might open your eyes as you open the Word.

highlight what "pops"

As you are in the Word, underline whatever pops out at you. In that first talk I heard on prayer,[3] Becky Tirabassi encouraged us to do this. At first I was a little "freaked out," but I did as she said and have never regretted it or turned back since. Over the course of a year, as I underlined the Scripture verses that popped out, I was excited to see a definite theme.

take note

Once you have underlined the Scripture verses
that stand out for you, go back and meditate on
them. Say them out loud; pray about them. Ask
the Holy Spirit to help you understand what he
is telling you through these words. This understanding may occur within minutes or it may
develop over time. Make a note of the date and
circumstances in the margin of your Bible.

God speaks

Start a journal or a section in your journal in which to record
the Scripture verses and themes that God brings into your
life. I use a simple collegiate binder with dividers. Some of
my friends use file cards, which they then carry around
with them, while others record them on
their computer. Experiment a little
and discover what is most effec-
tive for your personality. Ask
God to help you hear what he
is saying to you.

choices

What part of the Bible should you read? You have many different options. Some read a few Psalms and Proverbs every day. You might want to read the Scripture surrounding the sermon series at your church. If you are new to being in the Word, a great starting place is the book of John. (Try reading one chapter a day.) Pray that the Lord would guide you to your best starting place.

faith *from* hearing

The Bible comes in recorded formats as well as written. If listening to the Word of God is more "doable" for you, then by all means make your time investment there. Listen to your daily Word as you commute, walk, or sit in your favorite quiet spot. Pause and record that which pops out at you and then pray and meditate on it.

Faith comes from hearing the message, and the message is heard through the word of Christ.

ROMANS 10:17

growing appetite

Are you having a case of the "I don't wanna's"? Do you often find that you are not in the mood to read the Bible, that you don't understand what you are reading in the Bible, and frankly it isn't all that interesting to you? Then pray that God would grow in you an appetite for his Word. Pray that he would help you hunger after his laws and precepts and that when you read them, you would gain understanding and satisfaction.

How sweet are your words to my taste, sweeter than honey to my mouth! I gain understanding from your precepts; therefore I hate every wrong path.

PSALM 119:103–104

meaning

Just because it pops off the page, doesn't mean that the meaning or teaching of Scripture will pop immediately into your heart. There are times when you may only understand as you prayerfully meditate, asking the Holy Spirit to teach you. Other times you will need to reread your underlined verses several times, look them up in different translations, and even check the notes in a Bible for further insight. So when you lack clarity or understanding, go to God in prayer.

"alert *to* life"

Florence and Marita Littauer, who have trained thousands of Christian speakers and writers through their ministry at CLASS, promote the idea of staying open to everything and looking for lessons. Be "alert to life" today, and as you encounter recurring themes either through songs, quotes, stories, a person's encouraging words, a sermon...record them in a journal with your daily Scripture verses. Ask God for wisdom in applying these lessons.

be prepared

Bring your Bible with you to church along with a pen and paper. As you listen to the message, follow along in your Bible, taking notes, underlining, and prayerfully asking the Holy Spirit to speak to you through the teaching. By carrying your Bible with you, you are in essence preparing to listen and learn. You are tuned in.

no shame

Use the table of contents in the front of your Bible and stop being intimidated by the people around you who seem to find Scripture references in seconds. Give yourself permission to have a "learning curve." There is no shame in admitting what you do not know. Pray and ask God to gently remind you that you are never finished learning.

research

If you are struggling with a particular issue (anything from fear to finances), the best place to go is God's Word. Look up in the concordance (often located in the back of the Bible) key words that relate to your concerns. As you read these verses, ask the Holy Spirit to give you understanding.

Your word is a lamp to my feet and a light for my path.
PSALM 119:105

"how do you say my name?"

One night at bedtime, Spencer, who was five at the time, began to pray, "Our Father who art in heaven, how do you say my name?" After a good laugh and a bewildered look from Spencer, I pondered the depth of his question. How does God say my name? Quite frankly it is mind-boggling that God even knows my name! Yet he does. And he knows your name. Spend a few minutes looking up Isaiah 43:1–13; Revelation 2:17; and Revelation 3:5. Thank God that he knows your name.

a daily word

If you are a mom, you are probably standing at the sink most of the day either getting a meal ready or cleaning up after a meal. Invest in a daily calendar that has Scripture on it so that you can take in the Word when you are standing at the sink. If there is a different location in your house where you find yourself for extended periods of time, place the calendar there (your bathroom as you dry your hair, next to the chair where you breast-feed or rock your little one to sleep...). Let these Scriptures guide you into prayer.

out *and* about

Take a trip to the bookstore or the library and browse around while the kids read or play. Christian literature is a wonderful way to internalize God's truth. Ask a woman whose Christian walk you admire what books have most impacted her. Pray that God would guide you to the book that he wants you to read for the season that you are in.

share *the* wealth

It is exciting when God speaks to you in the details of your life. Share that enthusiastically! The old saying "Enthusiasm begets enthusiasm" applies here. People may decide to begin spending more time in the Word so that they can experience what you are experiencing. Pray that God would make you aware of what he wants you to share and with whom.

speaking *the* truth

Often when I am reading the Bible, God will place a particular person on my heart. I will become aware that a particular Scripture is for that person. What I usually do is write the Scripture out on stationery (which I always keep in the basket that holds my Bible and journal for just such an occasion) and sign it, "The Lord put you on my heart today." Some other options include sharing the verse over the telephone, in person, or via e-mail. Ask God to make you aware if there is someone he wants you to encourage today with his truth.

take your fingers
out of your ears

I stood at the sink, up to my elbows in dish soap, as I told my three-year-old son why it was important for him to be a "first-time listener." As I continued with what I thought to be a very good teaching about obedience, I looked down at him and noticed that he was looking at me with his elbows in the air and his fingers shoved in his ears. Aghast, I asked him, "What are you doing?"

In a very serious tone he replied, "I just wanted that sound to stop" (that sound being my voice). Has the Lord been speaking difficult truths to you through his Word, lessons that you would rather ignore? Has he been calling you to "come up higher" with him by living a holy, set-apart lifestyle and you would rather not listen? Ask God to forgive you for putting your fingers in your ears, and ask him for the grace and strength to be a "first-time listener."

who am I?

Between your role as a wife, a mother, a friend, a daughter…how often do you lose sight of who you are at your core? Look up these verses, underline them, and place a marker in these areas of your Bible so that you can be easily reminded of your true identity: Psalm 45:10–13; Psalm 139:13–16; 2 Corinthians 5:17; Ephesians 2:10; Colossians 3:12.

in full view

The book of Proverbs teaches, "A discerning man keeps wisdom in view" (17:24). *Webster's*[4] defines *discerning* as "revealing insight and understanding." If you want to be a woman who reveals insight and understanding, you must "keep wisdom in view." Give yourself the opportunity to become a discerning woman today by placing some Scripture before your eyes. Write a verse that God may be repeatedly bringing into your life on a large piece of paper and put it on the fridge. Pray for a "spirit of discernment."

"tell me *a* story"

My husband says that the main reason he is able to remember so many Bible stories is because of the many Arch books his mother read to him growing up (illustrated Bible stories published in the '60s and now available online). When my children were small, I asked my mother-in-law if I could borrow that crateful of books. I have been amazed at the way the Lord has used these books and others to teach me as I read aloud to my children. So sit down with the kids today and read out loud. Let them choose a few books, and you choose a few. Pray that you and your children would "hear" what God is telling you during this time.

growing down (roots)

If you find that you are struggling to be in the Word regularly, consider participating in a Bible study. Not only will you be held accountable to be in the Scriptures because you will need to do some homework, but you will have an opportunity to discuss what you are learning with others. This really gives God's truth a chance to take root and grow. In prayer, ask God if this is what he wants you to do at this time, and if so, which study and with which group.

by heart

Read Psalm 119 (the longest psalm) to grasp some of the amazing benefits of the Word of God. One of those benefits is found in verse 11: by hiding the Word in your heart that you might not sin against God. Begin hiding the Word in your heart today by memorizing a short verse of Scripture. Write the verse out on a note card and carry it with you, saying it out loud several times during the day.

encouraging truth

Where were you on 9/11? I was sitting in my living room chair watching in horror as the second plane smashed into the World Trade Center. Later that day I took my daughter to dance class. I brought my *One-Year Bible* with me and opened it to that day's reading, which said, "Do not be afraid that some plan conceived behind closed doors will be the end of you. Do not fear anything except the LORD Almighty. He alone is the Holy One. If you fear him, you need fear nothing else. He will keep you safe" (Isaiah 8:12–14 NLT). Pray that God will keep you in his Word so that you can be encouraged and be an encourager to those around you.

leaving *a* legacy

Keep in mind that as a mother, little eyes are always watching you. Do they see you go to God's Word when you are troubled? Do they hear you claim God's promises when you are shaken? Do they hear you say things like "That reminds me of a story Jesus tells in the Bible"? Today sit down near your children with your Bible, and when they ask what you are doing, explain to them that you are "listening to the Lord." Pray that you and your children will listen to God all the days of your lives.

be specific

Praying specifically has been eye-opening and faith-growing to me. As I stepped out in faith, believing that God cared about everything that concerned me, I found, through the Word, answers to questions, encouragement, and love. Today be as specific as possible in your prayers. When you turn to the Word, look with expectation for answers to those prayers. Praise God as he meets you in the small questions and large concerns of your life.

pray along *the* way

As you read or study the Word today, pause and pray the verse or theme that resonates with you. For example, when you read Psalm 34:12–13: "Whoever of you loves life and desires to see many good days, keep your tongue from evil and your lips from speaking lies," you can pray, "Yes, Lord, I do love life, and I need you to help me to keep my tongue from evil. Place your hand over my lips in the moment before I am about to speak lies. In Jesus' name. Amen."

a verse *to* meditate upon

"Were not our hearts burning within us while he talked with us on the road and opened the Scriptures to us?"

LUKE 24:32

"I love you"
and
"do not fear"

"You are mine" and "I am near"
All these truths I get to hear
On Holy Pages they appear

prayers *that* start *with* your pen

There is power and passion in
penning your prayers.
It is your heart's cry on paper.

Writing my prayers down has kept me awake and "on task." It has also made me aware of thoughts and feelings that I had previously been blind to, and it has been a catalyst in growing my faith as I have watched the Lord answer and address these "penned" prayers. I believe the most precious thing that has occurred as a direct result of writing my prayers down, however, is that it has enabled me to be more present with my children.

Each day when I turned to the gratitude section of my journal and put my pen to the page, I became aware of the blessings before me. I wrote down all that I was thankful for and discovered in the process that it was mostly the little things:

> *Holding Spencer in my arms in the morning after he*
> *demanded, "Tuddle me!" through his pacifier.*
> *Grace's big blue eyes gazing at me steadily as she drank*
> *from her bottle.*
> *The feeling of a little body sitting on my lap as I read*
> *story after story.*
> *The sweet scent of sleepy heads when I got them from*
> *their cribs in the morning.*
> *The image of a little body in a fuzzy yellow sleeper*
> *waddling down the hall with a too-full diaper.*

The firsts and the funnies, the big accomplishments (first step, first tooth) and the little things my children said and did that kept me in stitches appeared on the page. Through the act of writing, the Lord increased my awareness of the abundant blessings he presents me with each moment of each day. This motivated me to be on the lookout for these special and fleeting blessings so as not to miss them. I wanted to receive all the Lord was giving me through my children and through my life. In order to do that, I needed to be present. Putting my pen to paper in prayer accomplished this in my life.

scriptural prayer

Search me, O God, and know my heart; test me and know my anxious thoughts. See if there is any offensive way in me, and lead me in the way everlasting. PSALM 139:23-24

get *it* down

Grab a pen and a piece of paper and write down the first five things that come to your mind for which you are grateful. Do this quickly and without self-criticism. This is one way to pray: *Thank you, God. I acknowledge the gifts you have given me.*

use your present

It seemed like every time I went to a retreat or a shower, someone handed me a beautiful ribbon-clad journal, which I promptly set aside to use someday when I had something "important" to write in it. How many journals have you received in your lifetime? Pull out one of those journals and put it next to your bed. When you see it, open it up and write down one or two things you can thank God for.

holy conversation

Becky Tirabassi[1] is a huge advocate of writing your prayers. She recommends writing out (longhand) the words of Psalm 139:23–24 on a daily basis and then waiting for the Lord to bring to mind that which needs to be confessed. This has been a humbling yet freeing exercise for me. As I place my sin upon the page, I get it out of me and into the light of God's grace. He is then able to transform, exhort, and direct my steps, all the while communicating to me that he died for my sins past, present, and future. Write the verse out yourself (refer to the scriptural prayer) and then write down what comes to you, asking God for wisdom.

lists

List-making can be an act of prayer. Let go of all of the "rules." Do not concern yourself with grammar, punctuation, or the order in which the thoughts come to the page—just begin. You can use Praise, Confession, Thanksgiving, and Intercession as possible titles or headings for your lists. Even a "To-do" List can be an act of prayer as you ask God to help you know what he wants you to do.

dear God

When I was a little girl, one of my favorite people was a blind priest by the name of Father Patrick Martin.[2] After years in ministry, he began to write a letter to God each day. This exercise completely transformed his life and deepened the level of intimacy he experienced with the Lord. Write a letter to God and tell him everything you feel today. What do you need from him? What are the burdens that you desire to lay at his feet? Is there anything you feel grateful for that you want to mention to him? Get it all down in the form of a letter.

dear child

Place your pen on the page and ask God what he wants to tell you today. Start writing (even if it feels awkward), keeping in mind that this is for your eyes only. God's Word states, "Neither death nor life, neither angels nor demons, neither the present nor the future, nor any powers, neither height nor depth, nor anything else in all creation, will be able to separate us from the love of God that is in Christ Jesus our Lord" (Romans 8:38–39). Knowing the truth of these verses, always include somewhere within the lines of your letter these words from your Father: "I love you."

examine gratitude

The next time you find yourself waiting for the doctor with your child, use the paper that covers the examination table to "journal" with your child. Talk about what you are grateful for and take turns writing those things down in two lists. If you have a young child, ask him or her to draw a picture of what he or she is thankful for, and then you try to guess what it is. You have a captive audience, so start praying on the exam table!

journaling *with* junior

A few weeks ago the search was on for our neighbor's puppy. The kids gathered around our kitchen table to make "Lost Dog" signs to post around the neighborhood. In the meantime my son found the puppy asleep under a sofa cushion. The kitchen table kids promptly turned their signs over and wrote thank-you letters to God. My seven-year-old wrote, "God, thank you for giving Spencer the mind to find Cassie Conrad." Who says the kids can't participate? Have your kids draw a picture or write a prayer to God.

pick *a* prayer day

Write prayers for different members of your family on different days of the week. Perhaps you will choose the person according to which practice you will be waiting at that day. For example, if you sit outside the gymnastics studio for an hour on Mondays while your daughter takes a lesson, you can pray for her during that time, while Wednesdays you pray for your son as you wait during his soccer practice. Today as you write your prayers, focus in on one of your children.

what lurks beneath?

For the first few years of journaling, I used the "list" technique, which was very helpful for me, especially when my attention span lasted about as long as my children's did. But then the Lord began to nudge me to write in more of a stream-of-consciousness style rather than in lists. I resisted, thinking that I wasn't going to "do it right" as far as the grammar and punctuation were concerned. But the more I thought about it, the more I realized that what I was most afraid of was what would "come up" on the page. What feelings and thoughts was I hiding, even from myself? Do you have any fears like this? Pray for the boldness and courage to allow whatever is there to come to the surface, keeping in mind that "there is now no condemnation for those who are in Christ Jesus" (Romans 8:1).

only God sees

My daughter handed me a piece of construction paper with the words "ONLY GOD SEES" scrawled in large black letters. The truth of this hit me hard. Today write out that which you have felt the most hurt by in your lifetime. Was it the rejection you experienced in school? The abuse you experienced at the hand of a family member? The absence of encouragement and affection in your childhood? It may have happened this week, last month, or years ago. Tell Jesus everything in as much detail as possible. When you are finished, write this verse at the bottom of the page in bold letters: "YOU ARE THE GOD WHO SEES ME" (Genesis 16:13). Write it again. Let the truth of it sink in.

anger outlet

I spent many years perfecting my role as "the nice girl who was never angry" in an attempt to earn the love of others and God. When I finally understood God's unconditional love for me, I felt freed to look at many things in my life, including my anger. My journal gave me a safe place to contain the anger. Is there any anger in you? Bitterness? Unforgiveness? Get it out of you and onto the page. Anger has a way of seeping out in surprising ways when you try to "keep a lid on it," so be honest with yourself and with God. You can rip up the page later if it will make you feel any better.

disentangle

Have you ever felt "down" and not been aware of the reason? Depressed, with seemingly no cause? Take twenty minutes to write down what you are feeling, even if it is frustration with the fact that you have no idea what the problem is. Pray that the Lord will meet you during this time and minister to the "sinking" part of you.

"Thoughts disentangle themselves when they pass through your fingertips."[3]

handing *it* over

Place the numbers 1 to 10 on a blank sheet of paper. As fast as you can, write out ten things you feel concerned about today. They can be "VIP" or seemingly insignificant; just take the time to put them on the page. Now look up Psalm 55:22. Read it and then write it at the bottom of the page. Rewrite this verse in your own words. Hand over your concerns to the One who cares.

a gift *of* hope

Buy separate journals for each of your children and record your prayers for them there as well as your thoughts, feelings, hopes, and dreams. This is a place where you can write the prayers that you may not see answered for years to come (for a spouse, career...). You can even write letters to your children here for them to read at a future date.

go fishing

Are there people in your life you would like to see come to a personal relationship with the Lord Jesus Christ? Write their names down on a piece of paper and keep it in your Bible or another place where you might be reminded to pray for them. Years ago our pastor handed out pieces of paper that were cut in the shape of fish and had us do just this. He also had us pray for opportunities to communicate personally the Good News of Jesus with these people.

prayers *for the* new year

At the beginning of the year, I get out a clean sheet of paper and write down my prayer requests for the year. These prayers include one or two things that I would like to see the Lord grow in my life and the lives of my family and friends. Each day I pray down this list, and as answers come, I circle the request and place the date or a note next to it. As the year comes to a close, I look back in wonder at all that the Lord has done. It is quite a faith-building activity! Get out a sheet of paper and start your list... it doesn't even have to be January 1!

praise *the* Lord

Write down as many characteristics of God that you can think of (loving, faithful, mighty, holy). When you are finished, go down the list, saying each word out loud. I am always taken aback at the power there is in simply speaking who God is. With pen in hand, catch your feelings on paper after you have praised the Powerful One.

free indeed

Write down the worst thing(s) you have ever participated in—the sin that nobody knows about. Maybe it was a sin that was done to you and yet somehow you are the one that carries the shame. Place that shame on the page. Then get a red marker and put a giant diagonal line through it, writing over the top of that page: "If I confess my sins, he is faithful and just and will forgive me my sins and cleanse me from all unrighteousness." (Based on 1 John 1:9.) Say out loud, "Thank you, Jesus. In faith I choose to believe that I am forgiven because of what you did on the Cross for me. I choose to forgive myself, and I choose to believe that I am free indeed." Rip up that paper into small pieces, throw it away, and walk in the freedom and forgiveness that is yours.

family journal

Our women's ministry director told a group of us that when her children entered adolescence and communication became a bit more "strained," she began a family journal. She would write to her kids and leave the journal on their pillow. They would respond, and leave it on hers. Start your own family journal. If the kids are too small to write letters, they can still draw pictures in it, and you can read your letters and prayers aloud to them.

prayer requests

A few summers ago I led a group of women through a book called *The Path*,[4] which is about writing mission statements. At the end of the study, we all wrote down specific prayer requests that would help us accomplish our mission, and we agreed to pray for one another. It was a vulnerable and powerful experience to pray specifically for others and to be the recipient of specific prayers. Write down the prayer requests that you would like your friends to know and pray about for you.

signed, sealed, *and* delivered

Write a note or a card to a friend or family member and tell them what it is you are praying about for him or her that day. You can do this the old-fashioned way with a stamp, or you can use e-mail.

picture prayers

When I think of how far behind I am with my scrapbooking, I can become quite overwhelmed. I take comfort in the fact that when my children leave for college, I will be able to grieve and reminisce at the same time as I finally put their albums together. For those of you that do keep up with your scrapbooking, try journaling your prayers right onto the page next to the photographs.

lunch box love

Send your children off to school today with your prayers. Get a little piece of paper and write down your prayer for them today, or write it straight on the napkin that they will use to wipe their hands. If they can't read yet, you can draw a picture or put symbols (hearts, sunshine, crosses, x's and o's), or perhaps you can count on the teacher to read the prayer out loud to your little one as she puts straws in juice boxes and opens up applesauce containers.

what I want them *to* know

What do you want your children to know and never doubt? When I was thinking about this, I wrote a poem (featured at the end of this section). I framed it and put it in a place where I was sure they would read it every day...the bathroom! Get a piece of paper out and write down all that you want your children to know and never doubt. Over the next week, see if you can find Scriptures related to these themes. Pray and ask God how you can communicate this creatively to your kids.

my version *of the* truth

Rewrite a psalm or one of your favorite Scripture verses in your own words. Then write down the opposite of that verse. When I wrote the opposite of Philippians 4:6–7, I learned a lot about what NOT to do: "Do not be calm about anything, but in everything, continuing to grasp at control and busyness, with an entitled attitude, keep your worry to yourself. And the stress and anxiety that overwhelms and suffocates will eat away at your heart, your mind, and your very existence." No thanks! I'd rather do what God's Word tells me to do. Pray that this exercise will help you to see that God's way is always better than your own way.

a verse *to* meditate upon

Do not be anxious about anything, but in everything, by prayer and petition, with thanksgiving, present your requests to God. And the peace of God, which transcends all understanding, will guard your hearts and your minds in Christ Jesus.

PHILIPPIANS 4:6–7

you *are a*
child *of* God...

Wonderfully made
Faithfully guided
Continually helped
Always pursued
Never alone
Forever loved
A child of God!

7

prayers *that* start *with* romance *in* mind

> *Real prayer comes not from gritting our teeth but from falling in love.*
> —**RICHARD FOSTER**[1]

Flanked by two younger women and using her cane, the woman made her way toward me as I stood at the door following a speaking engagement. She arrived, a beautiful little grandma with short gray hair and penetrating eyes. Peering at me, she announced, "I am a pastor's wife two times over! I've traveled to six different states over the years, planting churches!"

I gave her a hug and responded, "Then you probably have some words of wisdom for this pastor's wife!"

With a twinkle in her eye and determination in her voice she began, "Love your family. Love your kids and your husband, but love your husband the most." She continued by addressing the talk she had just heard me present. "I liked how you carried the petunia image throughout your presentation. You should always wear pink—you look good in it; oh, and another thing, always have flowers with you. It draws people in."

She moved in a little closer, placed her free hand on my arm, and said quietly, "Every church is full of the same people. People change churches all the time looking for the perfect church, but they'll never find it because the same people are everywhere. It doesn't matter where you go, you'll always have that one person who complains no matter what you do or don't do, so take what people say

with a grain of salt. The most important thing is for you to love your family, but love your husband the most!" I nodded, taking in these profound truths. Even as I stood there, I realized that it would only be through the power of prayer that I would be successful in making this wisdom a reality in my life.[2]

scriptural prayer

Father God, your Word tells me, "Observe how Christ loved us. His love was not cautious but extravagant. He didn't love in order to get something from us but to give everything of himself to us. Love like that" (Ephesians 5:2 THE MESSAGE). Equip and enable me to do what you are calling me to do. Help me to "love extravagantly."

protected

When I look back over my life, I am amazed at all the times I could have been seriously hurt but was spared. God kept me from harm even when I was not aware of him or I was choosing to ignore and/or reject him. Can you recall moments in your life when you made a foolish choice and yet you were spared? As they come to mind, write them down in your journal and then write a prayer of thanks to your Protector, the One who fights for you. Isn't that romantic?

The LORD your God himself will fight for you.
DEUTERONOMY 3:22

pursued

One of my favorite themes in romantic movies is "the pursuit." In these movies the man will at all costs (even rejection!) continue to go after the woman to show her his love and devotion. This is a biblical theme as well. (See the book of Hosea.) God the Father continually demonstrates his love and devotion to us. How has God done that in your life? How has he been pursuing you? Spend a few minutes thanking him for his persistence.

tender truth

I was at a conference listening to Brennan Manning speak on the topic "Healing Our Image of God and Ourselves," when he said, "You are always being gazed at with infinite tenderness." The thought that God was not mad at me or looking at me disapprovingly when I made a wrong choice altered the way I saw everything from that moment on. Meditate on this tender truth today.

romantic

Write down five things that you personally
consider romantic. Moonlight walks, little
gifts that communicate "He knows me," long
conversations that include eye contact, help
with household chores, dinner and a movie...
Pray that the Lord will help you become
acquainted with your romantic side.

holding hands

Grab your husband's hand the next time you are walk-
ing and pray that there might be more romance in your
relationship. Often we as women wait for our men to
make the first "romantic" move, and we read all kinds
of things into it when they don't. Instead,
reach out to your husband, and
say a simple prayer for a
strong marriage.

safe harbors

Following our wedding ceremony, Russ and I became very successful at avoiding conflict. This led to distance and uncertainty. Thankfully, God brought us to a church that valued relationships. We began to meet weekly with five other couples who were committed to Christ, their marriages, and to one another. It was a safe place for us to begin to communicate with others about the joys and challenges of our marriage. Pray for a "safe harbor" for your marriage.

no D word

The pastor's wife had gathered us together moments before the wedding began. She invited us to give my sister words of encouragement and advice for marriage. She started us off with: "Never use the *D* word. Do not even let divorce be an option for you to think about, and certainly never speak about it." Pray about this. How has divorce affected your life? Consider making a fresh commitment to Christ to honor marriage by removing this word from your vocabulary.

on *the* rocks

You may have read the previous paragraph and become discouraged because your marriage and your heart lie broken "on the rocks." Take heart. Jesus says in God's Word, "'Everything is possible for him who believes'" (Mark 9:23). Confess any unbelief that you may be experiencing, and tell Jesus right now that you choose to believe him for your marriage. In this way you will begin to build your faith on the firm foundation of God's truth.

a new attitude

I came into our marriage with an underlying disdain and distrust of men. As the Lord continued to show me his unfailing love and unchanging grace, he began to heal the wounds that had caused these negative attitudes to grow. Then there came a day when he called me to repent—to turn from these sinful attitudes and to turn toward love. Is there any disdain in your life for your husband or for men in general? Make a list of the men in your life—past and present. Next to each name write the ways you were helped by that individual. Then go back and write down the ways that you were hurt. Pray about the ways these incidents have affected your life and your faith. Pray for continued healing for these hurts and for a new attitude.

lifted up

I love to listen to Grandma Harriet. This ninety-nine-year-old woman still gets stars in her eyes when she speaks of the man she called "husband" for fifty-five years. Although he passed away twenty years ago, she still says, "I *had* the love of *my* life." Listening to Harriet inspires me to speak about my husband like this. Pray that the Lord would give you the eyes to see the blessing your husband is and remind you to build up your husband with your words, even in his absence.

build your house

Draw a simple house in the middle of a piece of paper. At the top of the page, write the words of Proverbs 14:1 and under this list the ways you "tear down your house" (attitude, harsh words). At the bottom of the same page, write out the words to Psalm 127:1. Then make a list that starts at the bottom and moves up the page and into the house of all of the ways that you can "build up your house" (saying "I'm sorry," speaking encouraging words, prayer, time in the Word). Turn your home and heart over to the Lord in prayer.

loving him *the* most

Many a night when my children were little, I fell into bed exhausted from feeling "needed." Inevitably, it would be on these nights that my husband would want to be close to me. I had to pray that the Lord would help me to differentiate his needs from my children's needs. I also began to pray that the Lord would help me to have more desire and passion for my husband. Pray that the Lord will do the same for you.

waiting patiently

It was my prayer for a long time that Russ would initiate regular times of prayer for us as a couple. We were both praying and in the Word consistently, but separately. We attended a couple's retreat where an older gentleman from our congregation exhorted the men to pray over their wives, cleansing them with the Word of God on a daily basis. Russ began to initiate prayer slowly, and now we pray regularly together. (Praise God!) Pray for patience and for God's timing with your husband and prayer.

change him

How many of your prayer requests for your husband have been on the topic of changing him? Instead of asking God to change your spouse, ask God to increase your capacity to love your husband. Ask the Lord to shed light on any area in you that needs to change in order to make your marriage all God wants it to be. Consider going to your husband and asking him to forgive you for the ways that you have hurt him.

ask *and* tell

In the morning before you part ways, ask your husband if there is anything that he would like you to pray about for him that day. If he doesn't have an answer for you, tell him you'll let the Lord guide your prayer. If he does have an answer, ask him if he'd like you to pray for him right then and there or if he would prefer that you pray for him later on your own.

advice from "the coach"

Arguably the most well-respected basketball coach of our time is UCLA's John Wooden. In his book *Personal Best*[3] he writes, "The greatest thing a father can do for his children is to love their mother." For women, love can come pretty naturally, but respect can be more challenging. So if we were to apply Wooden's concept to mothers, I believe it would read, "The greatest thing a mother can do for her children is to respect their father." Take a minute to confess the ways you have failed to show your husband respect. Ask that the Holy Spirit would grow this romance-building and family-building trait into your heart.

> *However, each one of you also must love his wife as he loves himself, and the wife must respect her husband.*
>
> **EPHESIANS 5:33**

"I just called *to* say..."

When the two of you were dating, did you enjoy lingering over long phone conversations? These days I am guilty of calling Russ to ask for a favor more often than simply to encourage him. I have to be very intentional about leaving a message of respect and love for him during his work day. Pray and ask the Lord to tell you what you can do today to communicate respect and love to your husband.

remember when

Do you and your husband have a special song? Find that song and play it again. Really listen to the words of the song and let them lead you to pray for your marriage.

a little "getaway"

One of my favorite memories in our marriage occurred when we attended a Family Life Event called "Rekindling the Romance." What a blessing it was to worship the Lord together, pray together, and learn how we can build an even stronger relationship with each other. Pray about "getting away" and then research your options. Some places to begin your search include your own place of worship (many churches have couples retreats), *www.familylife.com* ("Weekend to Remember"), *www.loveandrespect.com*, and *www.family.org*.

"pre-prayer"

For many reasons my husband was not thrilled about the idea of attending a marriage conference when I first mentioned it to him, but after a few conversations and a lot of prayer, we did indeed sign up. Begin praying now about every aspect of your "getaway." Pray for soft hearts, for the best timing to talk about it, and for the words to say, and even pray for the resources that would enable you to attend (baby-sitter, finances, transportation).

lay *it* down

What are you being called to "lay down" today in your marriage? Is it something small, like how your husband loads the dishwasher? Is it something a little bigger, like laying down your preference of where you will go on vacation this year? Or perhaps it feels much heavier, like the bitterness that remains in your heart from broken promises. Ask God to reveal what it is that he is calling you to lay at his feet. Then lay it down in prayer.

listen up!

"Your husband is never your enemy!" Dennis Rainey's words rang through the Arrowhead Pond. I wrote those words down and have never forgotten them. Pray that the Lord would keep you alert to the enemy at work in your marriage. When you are in the middle of a disagreement or you are feeling angry or hurt, remember to pray, "Lord, what is going on here? Is there more here than meets the eye?" Rebuke your true enemy, the devil, with the authority that is yours through Jesus.

Submit yourselves, then, to God. Resist the devil, and he will flee from you. Come near to God and he will come near to you.

JAMES 4:7–8

excellent focus

Make a list of "excellence" about your spouse, praying that the Lord would magnify those qualities in your eyes. Write out Philippians 4:8 ("Whatever is true, whatever is noble...") and beneath it write all of the qualities that first attracted you to your husband as well as the areas that he has grown in.[4]

bosom buddies!

Get connected. Spend time with godly women who are "for" your marriage—women who love you both and who will give you grace and truth. *Praying Wives Club* by Marita Littauer[5] is an excellent book that will guide you in the process of creating a place to pray with these friends. Likewise, encourage your husband to spend time with godly men.

declare what is *to* be!

There is no "magic" potion that transforms a marriage, but there is a powerful action you can take. Set the timer for five minutes and write down as many affirmations as you can (we have a great marriage, we support and encourage each other) and then declare them boldly, praying that they would become a reality in your marriage.

stop fighting
and start writing

I have found the verse "Do not let the sun go down while you are still angry" (Ephesians 4:26) to be particularly challenging, especially when Russ and I seem to be "missing each other." One thing that has been helpful for us is to "write it down." I have gone to my journal and gotten my feelings out there and prayed. I have also received letters from Russ that have helped me to see him better. Pray for the ability to listen the next time you argue with your husband. Pray that the Lord would help you know if you need a "time out" to stop fighting and start writing.

When words are many, sin is not absent, but he who holds his tongue is wise.

PROVERBS 10:19

chalkboard prayers

Get a white board or chalkboard that you can hang up in your home. Ours is in the bedroom next to the dresser (the place Russ unloads his pockets). Write your prayers and encouragements for your husband on this board, starting today.

"into-me-see"

Before my first writers' conference I felt that the Lord wanted me to ask Russ to pray over me specifically for the conference. It was a very humbling and intimate thing for me to ask of him. I've heard the word *intimacy* explained as "into-me-see." When a specific circumstance or issue comes up in your life, humbly ask your husband if he would pray with you.

researching his needs

Have you ever asked your husband what actions communicate love and respect to him? Three books that have encouraged me to love my husband in ways that he can feel are *Wild at Heart* by John Eldredge,[6] *The Five Love Languages* by Gary Chapman,[7] and *His Needs, Her Needs* by Willard Harley.[8] Pray that the One who created your husband would help you to understand and love him even more extravagantly.

a verse *to* meditate upon

Honor one another above yourselves.
ROMANS 12:10

in my marriage
and in my home

Remind me, Lord, I'm not alone.

On those days when life's a mess
Help me lean on you for rest.

8

prayers *that* start *as* you partner *with* others

Our power is not so much in us as through us.

—**HARRY EMERSON FOSDICK**[1]

The summer before my son started kindergarten, I felt led to begin a prayer ministry for the children, the school, and the teachers. This was frightening for me, because while I had been praying consistently for many years by this point, I was not yet comfortable praying out loud in front of other people.

Nevertheless, using the tried and true format of the twenty-year-old ministry of Moms In Touch International, I began to gather in a weekly time of prayer with other moms.

Words cannot fully express what a blessing these meetings have been. They have been times of tears, triumph, and total surrender as we have bathed one another's children in prayer and stood side by side against the powers of evil over our school. Perhaps the most amazing time I have had in agreeing prayer occurred when I prayed with women I had never met and who lived a world away.

In September 2004 I listened in horror to the news. Terrorists had taken over an elementary school in Russia, holding hundreds of children and adults hostage. I left for a scheduled school meeting with a heart that was heavy, especially for the mothers of the hostages. Before the meeting began, we lifted up this crisis in prayer, praying specifically for those mothers whose hearts were breaking. We later learned that hundreds of lives were lost during this terror-filled ordeal that did not end for over fifty hours.[2]

A few months following this tragedy, I opened my Moms In Touch International newsletter and learned that there was a Moms In Touch group in Beslan, Russia, at that very school. The leader of that group, Bella Totiev, lost two daughters, three nieces, and a nephew during the takeover.

I read on as Bella Totiev's one surviving niece told of all the prayers that the Totiev children prayed throughout this frightening time, even teaching others (children and adults) to pray by writing out the Lord's Prayer on scraps of paper and passing them around the gym. The article stated, "In the midst of a terrible crisis, prayed-for children became prayer warriors themselves."[3]

As the mothers at our school prayed for this crisis, we had no idea that we were "agreeing" with mothers a world away. This is the power of agreeing prayer.

Christmas card kids

Save your Christmas cards and place them in a basket. After a family meal, have each of your kids choose a card from the basket and then spend a few minutes praying over that family. It's a simple way to "agree" in prayer as a family and to teach your children that prayer is a powerful and loving gift to give others.

new year agreements

Ask your friends and family members at the beginning of the year (or starting today) how you can pray specifically for them throughout the course of the year. Perhaps they are in the process of looking for a new home or trying to get pregnant. Whatever their needs are, you will be blessing the people in your life by agreeing with them in prayer.

e-mail agreement

Maybe your potential prayer partner lives many miles away. Pray for each other by using modern technology—the computer. My father-in-law recently told me that he received an e-mail from a friend for whom he had been praying. This fellow had been sick and was thanking his friends for praying. He ended the letter by writing, "There's no better place to be than in someone else's prayers!"

survival 101

We all have them—those moments when our anger and frustration reach the boiling point and we have a choice to make: either restrain the child or restrain ourselves! These are the moments to pray. It is difficult to walk away from these situations and seek the Lord, so I encourage you to call a sister in Christ and ask her to pray with you. Picking up the phone and praying with someone who cared was God's "Survival 101" lesson for me in those early years of motherhood.

channels of grace

God's grace has often come to me through relationships with other women. These were women who could laugh and cry with me about the ups and downs of motherhood, and women who were committed to Christ and to me. Pray about attending a group that will foster relationships with other Christian mothers. I recommend the following organizations:

MOPS (Mothers of Preschoolers) "A dynamic program designed to nurture mothers with children from infancy through kindergarten" (www.mops.org).

Hearts at Home has the mission of "meeting the needs of women in the profession of motherhood" (www.Hearts-at-Home.org).

Moms In Touch International is two or more moms who meet for one hour each week to pray for their children, their schools, their teachers, and administrators (www.momsintouch.org).

opening your mouth

"I'm a private person"; "I don't know what to say"; "I'm too self-conscious."

I've heard all of the excuses that keep people from praying out loud, and I've even said a few of them myself. Pray that the Lord would block everybody else out and give you the courage to open your mouth and release your prayers to him, even if it is just saying, "Yes, Lord," out loud, in agreement with the person next to you as he or she prays.

a prayerful embrace

The next time you see a friend or family member who is "looking low," give that person a hug and pray quietly for him or her during the embrace. A simple prayer that I have spoken in these circumstances is *Lord, I lift up my friend to you right now. I do not know what is troubling her, but I am thankful that you do. Meet her right where she is, Lord, and bless her, in Jesus' name. Amen.*

accountability

As the Lord makes you aware of specific areas of temptation in your life, pray for a safe person with whom you can share this. Talk through what would be most helpful for you. When she sees you wandering off the path, how can she hold you accountable? Are you a tell-it-like-it-is girl? Or do you prefer a more gentle approach?

Brothers, if someone is caught in a sin, you who are spiritual should restore him gently. But watch yourself, or you also may be tempted.

GALATIANS 6:1

mood swings

"I don't feel like praying." Today if this is true for you, call a friend or family member to pray over you, or pick up a favorite devotional/book by an author with whom you connect.

> *Into a man's prayerless mood let a little living water from someone else's prayer be poured, and water from the nether wells of the man's own soul may flow again.*
> —HARRY EMERSON FOSDICK⁴

café concerns

I recently met a darling southern woman named Regina who told me that when her pastor and his family are eating out, he always says to the waitress, "We're fixing to pray. Is there anything we can pray for over you?" Regina informed me with delight that he has yet to have a waitress refuse this. Are you feeling bold enough to offer to agree in prayer with your waitress? Perhaps a good start would be to pray in public as a family over your next meal out.

joining together

They all joined together constantly in prayer, along with the women and Mary the mother of Jesus, and with his brothers.

ACTS 1:14

In the preceding verse, "they" represents the apostles who joined with the "women" to pray. This was highly uncommon for this time in history. A simple way to begin to "join together" is to find a church home and commit to attending regularly. Pray that the Lord will guide you to this home.

prayer team

Many churches have a prayer team that meets regularly. Visit yours when you are in need or if you simply feel led to join them as they pray for the body of Christ.

facing opposition

When Peter and John began to preach the gospel, they were thrown into jail and told not to speak or teach at all in the name of Jesus. (See Acts 4:18–26.) Yet as soon as they were released, the two met with "their own people" and immediately "they raised their voices together in prayer to God." As you face opposition in your own life, pick up the phone, meet with a friend, or ask your spouse to pray with you.

propelled forward

This book came about as a result of prayer; therefore, it did not surprise me when the Lord called me to ask others to pray me through the entire process. I sent out over two hundred and fifty postcards asking friends and family to partner with me in prayer. That's when the doubts started coming: "What will people think? Will they think I'm bragging?" As I journaled these concerns, in my heart I heard God's response: *"This book is about the power of prayer, and it must be propelled forward on the energy of prayer—intercessory prayer."* Boldly ask for specific intercessory prayer today and watch as the power of Christ is released in your life.

don't miss it!

It is awesome to *see* prayers answered, but sometimes we miss it. We need to help one another see the answers. Ask a friend about the specific circumstances and people that you have been praying with her about so that you can praise God when you see and hear the answers.

international agreement

Agreeing in prayer is not limited to those times when we are in the same room with bowed heads. We can agree in prayer with those who are far away.

Many ministries have online "prayer partner" departments. Pray about becoming a prayer partner with a ministry.

mentors *and* motivation

My prayer life has been the most affected
through specific mentors in my life. These mentors have come in different forms—a relationship, a book, a teaching tape, a speaker. I have
needed these mentors to teach me how to pray
and to help me stay motivated to pray. Pray and
ask God to show you the mentors he has placed
in your life to help you stay motivated in prayer.

discipler

When I was at a speaker training, I met a delightful older
woman who exhorted us to teach others what the Lord had
taught us. She explained that just because we are young,
we need not assume we have nothing to offer someone
who is older than us. She finished by saying that we all
have different levels of maturity, and we can help one
another grow if we are obedient to share. Ask the Lord if
he has a certain person in mind that he would like you to
spend more time with, to pray with, and/or disciple.

book study

Pray about asking a friend to go through a Bible or book study with you. There are many great resources at your local Christian bookstore with easy-to-follow formats. All you need is a teachable spirit and an open heart. It will be a great opportunity to learn and grow as well as to give you an opportunity to pray specifically for each other.

meeting places

Make a list of the locations where you meet with your girl-friends (with or without the kids). Consider all of these locations as opportunities to "agree in prayer." It doesn't take long, and it doesn't have to be a specific time set aside to pray. Think of agreeing in prayer as a lifestyle.

Speak to one another with psalms, hymns and spiritual songs.

EPHESIANS 5:19

bumps, bruises, *and* broken hearts

In the evenings when I ask my daughter if she has any prayer requests, I am touched by the care and concern she has for the people in her life. We agree in prayer that her friend's cut would heal, that her daddy would come home safe from his trip, and that her brother would win his baseball game, and recently she asked me to pray that the Lord would comfort her and her brother because the neighbors were moving away. Life can be rough, even for kids. Join your little ones in prayer by asking them for their prayer requests and telling them something they could pray about for you.

always *in* fashion

Have you ever heard of a "prayer chain"? Many churches still employ this technique of intercessory prayer. Here is how it works: There is a list of phone numbers in a certain order, and when a prayer request comes in to the church, someone calls the first number, and that person makes one call to the next person on the list and so on until numerous people are praying for the specific circumstance. See if your place of worship has this system in place and consider becoming one of those prayer contacts. Perhaps you could start your own prayer chain if there isn't one at your church.

avoid godless chatter

Moms In Touch encourages groups to spend the entire hour praying. It is so easy to derail, believing that we need to explain our prayer requests in detail before we can begin praying. There are also times that even with the best of intentions when asking for prayer requests for a friend we divulge too much information. Ask the Lord to "place a guard over your mouth" that would keep you from idle talk as you partner with others in prayer.

Avoid godless chatter, because those who indulge in it will become more and more ungodly.

2 TIMOTHY 2:16

park *and* pray

One of the things I miss now that my kids are in school is the freedom I had in my schedule with them. Many a day came when the phone rang, and I heard, "How about we meet at the park in an hour?" I'd get the kids into their car seats and head out for some sunshine. It was space to play, pray, and just "be." Now that the kids are older, I have to be more intentional about scheduling play and pray time. Make a plan to meet a girlfriend at the park this week. When there is a quiet moment at the park, "agree."

conflict resolution

When you find yourself in a time of conflict in a relationship, let it be a reminder to pray. Suggest praying with the individual before you try to work it out. Invite Jesus into the conversation and ask him to help you truly hear each other and love each other.

the great physician

One day Peter and John were going to the temple to pray when they came upon a crippled man. He asked them for money, and this is how Peter responded: "Silver or gold I do not have, but what I have I give you. In the name of Jesus Christ of Nazareth, walk." (See Acts 3:1–10.) Follow the example of these two believers. When someone is sick, agree in prayer that in the name of Jesus he or she would be healed.

a blessing *in a* basket

I was traveling to a speaking engagement in San Diego. The day that I was leaving, I opened my front door to find a basket filled with my favorite snacks, brightly colored flowers, and a tiny gold frame with the words, "I fix my eyes on you, the Author of my faith." My dear friend Nancy truly "spurred me on" and encouraged me to stay in relationship with Jesus during my time away. Prayerfully ask God if there is someone you can "spur on" this week.

becoming that woman

I have been inspired by many "a woman of prayer" in my life, but one special lady inspired me to write the poem on page 189. Pray that you too would become a "woman of prayer," and in so doing inspire others to do the same.

a verse to meditate upon

> *"Ask and it will be given to you; seek and you will find; knock and the door will be opened to you. For everyone who asks receives; he who seeks finds; and to him who knocks, the door will be opened."*

MATTHEW 7:7–8

"a woman of prayer"

Talking to Jesus was her favorite release
It brought her comfort, purpose, joy, and peace

Softly and quietly uttering praise
Tearfully speaking of missing "the Way"

Battling, fighting, and holding her ground
As intercession poured forth and hope showered down

Affirming with Scripture what she knew to be true
This woman inspired all those she knew

With her passion for Jesus
And her love for his Word

And with fervent prayers
Which we're certain God heard

Many a girlfriend has earnestly shared
That they've followed her lead and become

a woman of prayer

9

prayers *that* start *when* God says, "go!"

*I myself do nothing. The Holy Spirit
accomplishes all through me.*
—WILLIAM BLAKE¹

A painting hangs on my dining room wall. It is a vibrant rendition of Jesus standing in an open doorway. Behind him are rows of tables set lavishly with crystal and china and loaded down with fruit, breads, and cakes. Hundreds of people sit around the tables talking animatedly to one another in the light-filled room. The scene evokes a sense of joy and celebration.

On the other side of the doorway, a barefoot man kneels in the snow, shivering in the dark of night. All you can really make out is a slight profile of his face, for it is his body that communicates what he is truly thinking. One of the man's hands points to his chest as if to say, "Me? Really?" while the other hand clasps tightly to the outstretched arm of Jesus. Jesus gazes intently and lovingly at the man, and with his free arm motions toward the party behind him. The piece, by artist Morgan Weistling, is called "The Invitation."

Yesterday, in prayer, I sensed God telling me to give this painting to my mother. My mother and I have experienced more than a little distance in our relationship in recent years, and quite frankly I am not certain that she will even like the painting. I, on the other hand, love it. So I am puzzled over God's urging on this. I also wonder if my mother will question my motives and have difficulty truly receiving the gift. At this stage in my walk with Jesus, however, I am

aware that it doesn't matter whether or not I have answers to my questions. What matters is that I have faith.

When I am on the listening end of prayer and God tells me to do something, my response needs to be obedience based on trust in my holy, loving, and wise Father. Over and over again I have been witness to the fact that, in the power of the Holy Spirit, I am able to accomplish that which God calls me to. So even though questions may still surface when I am listening to God, I know the best choice is to do what he says. I will give the painting to my mother and trust God's plan.

scriptural prayer

Lord, help me to remember that it is not by might, nor by power, but by your Spirit. When you say, "Go," please help me to trust you and move out empowered by your Spirit. When I get weary, help me call out for a fresh outpouring of your Spirit so that I can move on and affect the kingdom with godly action. In Jesus' name. Amen. (Based on Zechariah 4:6)

test it

God will never tell you to do something that is in disagreement with his Word. When you feel that you are "hearing" from God, test it against the Word. Ask God in prayer, "Is this really from you? Please show me clearly in the Bible what the truth is."

hugs *and* love

My five-year-old daughter repeatedly "bear-hugged" her baby cousin before saying to herself, "I just love her so much I can't stop hugging her." I was struck by the fact that this is how God feels about us. Ask God who needs a hug from you today, and as you act on it, remember that God loves you and can't keep his hands off you!

forgiveness

When you pray, "Search my heart, O God," does the same strained relationship come to mind? Write a letter today to that person, owning up to that for which you are responsible, communicating the ways you know you've hurt that person and asking for forgiveness. Maybe you need to forgive someone who has hurt you. In your letter, communicate that you forgive the person even if he or she is no longer living.

minister *to the* mission field

Ask your church about the missionaries your congregation is helping. In prayer, ask God how you can be an encouragement to them. Is it writing them a note of encouragement and/or sending them financial support? Using a map, show your children where these missionaries live and explain to them what a missionary does.

gift *of* grace

When I was a little girl, family friend Father Patrick Martin left me an unexpected surprise—a tape recorder that I had admired on one of his visits. I never forgot that gift of grace. If someone admires something that you own, prayerfully ask God if he wants you to give it to that person as a gift of grace.

phone *a friend*

Ask God if there is someone he wants you to reach out to. Call a friend and be an "active listener." Ask her how she is doing and then *really* listen. Offer an encouraging word here and there and then pray with your friend for a few minutes before you say good-bye. Show love with action.

> *Kind words can be short and easy to speak, but their echoes are truly endless.*
>
> —MOTHER TERESA[2]

open your hand

God doesn't need your money, he wants your heart. Pray and ask the Lord what he is calling you to give. Then open your hand and give him your heart today.

> *Each man should give what he has decided in his heart to give, not reluctantly or under compulsion, for God loves a cheerful giver.*
>
> 2 CORINTHIANS 9:7

a life-changing act

Our friend Scott was born with cystic fibrosis and lived a life marked by moments of great joy (marriage and the birth of his daughter) and tremendous sickness and hospitalization. His only hope of a cure was a full lung transplant. Through the generous action of another, Scott did receive his miraculous cure. Scott and his family now have a new beginning. Pray about becoming an organ and/or blood donor.

crisis hits

When you become aware of a crisis in the life of a friend, a relative, or even a stranger, ask the Lord how you can be of help. Is it visiting that person in the hospital? Is it organizing meals for the family? Is it driving someone to an appointment? Cleaning a friend's house? Be open to being a helper in times of crisis.

get *in the* water

Learning how to water-ski can be intimidating; fear can keep you standing on the dock. But if you really want to ski, you must get into the water, hold onto the handle, face the right direction, and wait. It is the power of the boat that will pull you up. The next time you feel frightened about doing something new, prayerfully reflect on Philippians 4:13 and then "get into the water" and wait for the power of the Holy Spirit to pull you up.

soccer walk

One of my girlfriends[3] travels on the weekends to her daughter's soccer tournaments. In her desire to see the game be injury free and full of good sportsmanship, she has taken to praying as she walks the perimeter of the field before each game. Ask God if there are any sports activities or other extracurricular activities (dance or music recitals, plays, other performances) at which you can pray and walk.

prayer secret

Have you ever been the recipient of an anonymous "random act of kindness"? Take a moment to think about how it made you feel to receive that blessing. In prayer, ask God if there is an anonymous blessing that he would like you to initiate.

extend *an* invitation

I am the kind of person who can get ahead of myself, so when it comes to sharing my faith, I can quickly become paralyzed. When I look to Scripture, I am comforted to see that Jesus didn't get ahead of himself; he simply said, "Come and see." Ask the Lord who he would like you to invite to church this Sunday.

Offer to pick up that person or tell him or her where you will meet.

special events

I went to preschool one day holding flyers for our upcoming women's retreat with the intention of inviting my new friend. But on that day a different woman initiated a conversation with me. As I stood there, I felt the Holy Spirit urging me to give her one of the flyers. A little confused, I gave her one, and she enthusiastically chose to attend. Over the course of a year I watched the Lord work in mighty ways in that woman's life. Are there any "outreach" events coming up at your church? Pray about asking a new friend or even an acquaintance to attend with you.

smile

My grandfather taught me: "A smile costs you nothing, but can mean everything to the person who is cheered up by it." Ask the Lord to tell you who could use a smile today. Is it the lady in the car next to you or the cranky cashier at the grocery store? Surrender your attitude to God and choose as an act of your will to say with a smile, "This is the day the LORD has made; let us rejoice and be glad in it" (Psalm 118:24).

words of life

Thinking back over your lifetime, what words have people said to you that felt "life-giving"? Did anyone, for example, ever say to you, "You were made for great things"? Write down those encouraging words you heard. Is it easier for you to remember the words that hurt you? Take a minute to think about the power words have. Pray that the Lord would place a guard over your lips and help you to speak only words that would build up. Ask God in prayer if there is someone specific who he wants you to "speak life to" today.

show up

I called my friend in tears. After spending two hours at the pediatrician's office (my fourth trip in two weeks) and getting breathing treatments for the baby, my car wouldn't start. I finally arrived home (after a stranger helped me get the car started) to burst into tears again. My two best friends were waiting for me, armed with flowers, French fries, and plenty of tissues. Pray and ask God who you need to "show up" for today. It might not seem like a big crisis to you, but it might mean the world to the one who is in it.

an extra helping

I have a sister who owns a restaurant, a mother who serves as the director of a food bank, and an uncle who likes to celebrate his birthday by cooking and serving a seven-course meal for twenty. It is no wonder that I love to nurture in this way as well. You don't have to be a gourmet cook to be a blessing. The next time you make dinner, double the recipe and ask God to whom you could take the extra helping.

minister *to the* minister

Ask God how you can support your pastor and his or her family today (or the worship team, associate pastor, school principal, teacher). Can you take their kids to the pool? Make them some brownies? Send some flowers or a restaurant gift certificate?

feeding *the* hungry

When you see a homeless person or someone who is in obvious need, ask the Lord if there is something he would like you to do for that person. Is it buying a meal for him or her at a fast-food restaurant? Is it offering the granola bar that you keep in your glove box? Is it giving money? Ask God in that moment. He'll tell you.

many gifts, one spirit

Read 1 Corinthians 12:4–11. What do you enjoy doing? What are your gifts? Is it singing? Painting? Working with numbers? Your gifts are vital, and they are a blessing to the body of Christ. Ask the Lord to reveal the gifts he has given you and to show you how he would like you to bring him glory through the application of those gifts.

divine appointment

"Divine appointments" is what I have heard them called. You are on a plane, and seated next to you is someone searching for hope and peace, or you meet a new mom at the park who has been thinking about going to church. Ask God to make you aware of "divine appointments," and then ask him in those moments what he wants you to do or say. It may be simply telling someone about the difference Jesus has made in your life.

do *the* right thing

The clerk miscalculated and gave you more change than you were due, or perhaps she failed to charge you for an item that you purchased. What do you do in these instances? Do you say, "No big deal" or "Thanks for the unexpected blessing, Lord!"? In moments like these, pray that the Holy Spirit would show you what the "right thing" is and enable you to do it.

To do what is right and just is more acceptable to the Lord than sacrifice.
PROVERBS 21:3

fasting

"But how will I make it through the day?" I asked myself when I felt the Lord calling me to give up my favorite caffeinated soda. This question exposed the reality—I was counting on something other than the Lord for energy and endurance. So with trepidation (and a few setbacks), I gave it up and realized anew my utter dependence on God. What is the Lord calling you to give up so that he can have his rightful position in your life and so that he can give you all that you need?

stay

The more I sought God in prayer, the more I became aware of the needs of the world and wanted to help meet those needs. Sometimes, though, with a sense of urgency, I moved out before I was supposed to, and in my own strength and power I made a mess of things. Save yourself (and others) a lot of pain by waiting for the Holy Spirit to empower you to accomplish God's plan. Ask God to show you clearly when you need to "go" and when you need to "stay."

I am going to send you what my Father has promised; but stay in the city until you have been clothed with power from on high.

LUKE 24:49

practice hospitality
(Romans 12:13)

Ask God if there is someone toward whom you can be hospitable. Is there a new couple who has recently begun coming to church? A mom who looks lonely at school? Invite them over for dessert or dinner. It doesn't need to be extravagant—you could even order pizza.

appropriate action

As I sat watching the movie *Because of Winn-Dixie,* I became aware of the little girl seated next to me. The little blond head buried in her hands couldn't hide the sound of tears. Her mother, a few seats away, was caring for a younger sibling and was unaware of the pain down the row. My first reaction was to wrap my arm around this child and comfort her, but I was a stranger to this precious one. I felt helpless. It was as I walked to the car later that it dawned on me that I could have prayed that the Lord would wrap his arms of comfort around the little girl. Through this incident, I learned that "prayer is the hug that is always appropriate." Pray and ask God who it is that is in need of a "prayer hug" today.

be present

Ever since I was a little girl, one of my favorite women was my aunt Tina. She always had time for me and made me feel special, even if it was just taking me with her to the grocery store. When she had children of her own, she also blessed them with her attention and presence. When I gave birth to Spencer and Grace, my aunt gave me an extraordinary gift—a framed poem (featured at the end of this chapter) that once hung on the wall of her home. It's a godly reminder for me to "go" and "be" with my children. Ask God what he wants you to set aside so that you can "go" and "be present" with your family.

a verse to meditate upon

> *Dear children, let us not love with words or tongue but with actions and in truth.*
> 1 JOHN 3:18

"excuse this house"

Some houses try to hide the fact
that children shelter there.
Ours boasts of it quite openly,
the signs are everywhere.
For smears are on the window,
little smudges on the door.
I should apologize, I guess,
for toys strewn on the floor.
But I sat down with the children
and we laughed and played and read.
And if the doorbell doesn't shine
their eyes will shine instead.
For when at times I'm forced to choose
the one job or the other,
I want to be a housewife
but first I'll be a mother.

—AUTHOR UNKNOWN

10 prayers *that* start *with a* hurting heart

When I am hurting,
my primary prayer is "Help!"

Standing in the church and looking at the words on the screen caused bitterness and disbelief to rise up within my heart.

"He's turned my mourning into dancing again. He's lifted my sorrow."[1]

With the sudden loss of my grandfather that week, I could not imagine how the Lord could possibly turn the ache I felt into some sort of exuberant dance celebration.

A few months before Grandpa's death, I had felt the Holy Spirit urging me to surrender everything that might be keeping me from serving the Lord wholeheartedly. The one thing that had always held me back was the incessant fear that God was going to take something away from me that I needed desperately. Nevertheless, on a January morning I surrendered it all in prayer—including this fear. Now I watched as my worst fear became a reality.

I attended our church women's retreat that fall with trepidation, still wandering through this new territory of grief. During the final moments of the retreat, the speaker encouraged us to pair off into groups and put a voice to the questions that we'd kept hidden from ourselves and others so that the Lord could, in his power, "help us with our unbelief."

As I sat with one of my dearest friends, I explained the betrayal I felt that when I surrendered everything to God, he took the one thing I needed the most—the man who had

been like a father to me. Yet the only place that I found any peace was in God's presence or in the presence of other believers. It was as I spoke that I remembered the truth in God's Word: All of our days are numbered and written in the book before the first one began. Words began to tumble from my mouth: "God knew that this was the day Grandpa was going to die! He didn't take him away from me; he prepared me for this day by drawing me so close to him that he could comfort me, and by surrounding me with so many brothers and sisters in Christ that I might not miss the touch of his Spirit on my life."

There did come a day when I stood with the congregation and sang the words to the song that had once made me so angry. While I did not know how, the Lord had "turned my mourning into dancing again. He lifted my sorrows."

scriptural prayer

Lord, I want to trust in you at all times. I want to pour my heart out to you, for you are my refuge. Your Word says that you hear me as I cry out and that you deliver me from all my troubles. I need you, Jesus. I need to feel your presence right here with me in my pain. (Based on Psalms 62:8 and 34:17–19)

get real

Even the psalmists said what was truly on their heart. In Psalm 88:18 we read, "You have taken my companions and loved ones from me; the darkness is my closest friend." God is strong enough to handle your emotions; he already knew what they were to begin with! So "get real" with God through prayer and allow the healing to begin.

things change

I resisted change for much of my adulthood. Only as I learned to lean on the One that is "the same yesterday, and today and forever" have I been able to handle change in my life. Pray to the immutable Lord as you face life's changes, asking him to uphold you with his right hand (Psalm 63:8).

permission

In the familiar passage of Ecclesiastes 3:1–8, we are taught that there is a time for everything, including "a time to weep and a time to laugh, a time to mourn and a time to dance." Pray that the Lord would help you to embrace the season you are currently in. God wants to comfort those who mourn, but many times in an effort to avoid the pain, we never enter into that season of mourning. Pray for the courage to enter and receive the blessing of Christ's comfort.

blessed rest

"You know you're tired when, within five minutes of waking up, you're planning when you can get your nap in." I laughed as my girlfriend said this to me during one of our early morning walks. Other than sleepless nights with newborns, seasons of suffering can be exhausting. Is there someone who can watch the kids for an hour so you can nap? Ask God to help you receive the sweet gift of rest today.

a woman of few words

At the time I heard Barbara Johnson speak, she had lost one of her four sons in the Vietnam War, another in a car accident, and had been estranged from another son for years. Yet she still sought the face of her Shepherd. Perhaps this is why I will never forget her advice to those ministering to a hurting friend: "When grief is the greatest, words should be the fewest." Pray that the Lord would direct you when to speak and when to remain silent as you walk through seasons of pain with your loved ones. If you are the one in that season, let people know what is and isn't helpful.

say thank-you

Continue the practice of prayerfully writing down that for which you are grateful. The night my grandpa died I wrote down everything I could think of about him that I was grateful for—from his enthusiastic hugs to his quiet acts of service to the poor. This entry became the eulogy that I gave at his funeral.

standing on God's promises

Start an ongoing "promise page" in your journal. On a sheet of paper, place the title "He Promises" and begin to record scriptural promises here. This will be a place for you to turn in times of trouble, doubt, and pain. You might want to begin with the promises included in Jeremiah 29:11, Philippians 4:13, Romans 8:28, and Isaiah 43:1–5.

My comfort in my suffering is this: Your promise preserves my life.

PSALM 119:50

listen *to the* little ones

Ask God to keep you open to the children in your life; they can be conduits of grace. After my grandfather passed away, my children really ministered to me through their words, especially my three-year-old, Grace. One morning when she woke up she told me that she had had a dream about Jesus. I asked her what Jesus was doing in her dream, and she said quite frankly, "He was taking care of Grandpa."

a sacrifice *of* praise

Praise God during this time, not because you want to or because you feel like it, but because he is worthy of our praise. The benefits of this sacrificial act are numerous, not the least of which is discovering as George Matheson did, "At last I truly know that I desire not the gift but the Giver."[2]

stay connected

In times of pain my natural tendency is to isolate myself.
Staying in relationship when I didn't feel I had anything to
offer taught me more about the grace and compassion of
Jesus Christ than just about anything. Ask Jesus to keep
you from isolating yourself. Ask him to help you receive
the love that comes from staying connected.

carried *to* Jesus

In the Bible (Mark 2:1–5) we read about four friends
who carried their sick friend to Jesus. When they got
to the house, it was so crowded they had to climb up
onto the roof, make a hole in it, and lower their
friend down on a mat to the Great Physician. When
Jesus saw the faith of the man's *friends*, he said to
the paralytic, "Son, your sins are forgiven." Keep
your hurting friends in your prayers. When you are
the one who feels too weary to pray, lie on the
"stretcher of faith" and allow your friends to carry
you to the Father in their prayers.

close *at* hand

Keep the resources that have ministered to you in the past close at hand. These might include favorite books, quotes, prayers, and Bible studies. Turn through the pages once more, listen to the song again, and watch the movie that reminds you of the bigger truth. Pray that the Lord would reveal himself to you through these resources.

new insight

Pray that God would guide you to resources that will minister to you in this season of your life. Two of my favorites include the daily devotional *Streams in the Desert* by L. B. Cowman and *A Grace Disguised—How the Soul Grows Through Loss* by Jerry Sittser.[3]

healing landscapes

If you had a choice between going to the mountains or going to the beach, which would you choose? Think about the places that you are drawn to, places that communicate hope and healing to you. Consider setting aside some time for a visit to a healing space and then pray for the courage to go.

at *a loss for* words

Go to your knees in prayer today. You do not need to have words. You do not need to have clarity. Just go to your knees trusting this verse: "The Spirit helps us in our weakness. We do not know what we ought to pray for, but the Spirit himself intercedes for us with groans that words cannot express" (Romans 8:26).

seek counsel

One of the ways the Lord has loved me and supported me through grief has been through the wise counsel of his people. Pray for wise counsel today. It may come through a friend, a pastor, or even a professional therapist.

natural consequences

After college I participated in behavior that I knew in my gut was wrong. The consequence was a depression so dark and deep that all I felt was despair. I called my dad, who drove twenty-six hours nonstop to bring me home. He had no condemnation for me that day, only excitement about my return. Ask the Lord to examine your heart today. Is any of your pain a result of your sinful choices? Turn to Jesus. He has no condemnation for you. He will save you and bring you home to himself.

he feels your pain

Recently my son forgot to remove his favorite collection of cards from his pants pocket, and as a result I washed the pants, cards and all. I felt sick thinking about how sad he was going to be. It was then that I realized this must be a taste of how God feels about me with some of the choices I make. He feels my pain, and yet he allows me to make the choice anyway, with the hope that I will learn. Think back to a time when you made a poor choice or a mistake. Prayerfully journal about it, asking God what he was allowing you to learn through it.

why do I keep doing it?

What are the behaviors in your life that you know are wrong but you keep doing anyway (gossiping, overspending, cursing)? True repentance is a realization that I have hurt the One who loves me the most. Because of that realization, I choose to turn from my behavior and back to God. Write down the specific sin(s) that you struggle with and your "felt" consequences. Pray for a heart of true repentance.

new habits

Even with a heart that is broken in repentance before God and surrendered to his way instead of our ways, life is not going to be "easy." Indeed, there are times when God performs a miraculous work and removes certain desires from us (glory be to God!), but more often we have some work to do (in the power of the Holy Spirit) to break bad habits and develop new ones. Pray that the Lord would give you the strength, endurance, and tools that you need to break a bad habit.

no such thing

I spent a lot of wasted years looking for the "preventative-pain formula for life." When I asked Jesus into my heart, my life changed forever, but I still had the lie that "I should never experience pain" lurking around in my head. In John 16:33 Jesus teaches: "In this world you *will* have trouble" (emphasis mine). Today read John 16:33 for yourself and "take heart" in prayer.

leaving *and* staying

One of my dearest friends just informed me that she and her family will be leaving our church. It seems that this is the year for "leaving," as I've watched numerous friends move on to new neighborhoods, to new churches, and to new lives apart from their marriages. I am left grappling with the desire to shut down so that I don't have to feel this pain ever again. But I am increasingly aware that while others are leaving all around me, Jesus calls me to stay. Are there any areas in your life where Jesus is calling you to "stay"? Pray to him about this today.

walking *by* faith *and* not *by* sight

When things are looking bleak and don't seem to be changing anytime soon, take a moment to look up Hebrews 11:1. Then put on some shoes and go for a walk, praying that as you physically and symbolically move forward, God will grow your faith.

heavenly hope

Write down what you imagine heaven will be like. We need to remind ourselves on a regular basis (especially in times of pain) that we are not home yet. Read John 14:1–3 and pray for a glimpse of heaven and a heart that looks forward to a homecoming.

be still

Are you "at the end of your rope"? Hudson Taylor
was so weak and feeble in the last few months of his
life that he told a friend, "I am so weak I cannot
write. I cannot read my Bible. I cannot even pray. All
I can do is lie still in the arms of God as a little child,
trusting Him."[4] Today let your prayer be in response
to Psalm 46:10: "Be still, and know that I am God."

open *and* obedient

A few years ago dear friends lost their energetic and enthusiastic three-year-old son in a tragic accident. His passing brought an entire congregation and community to their knees. While Jack lay in a coma at the hospital, Pastor Matt Stemme visited his parents. Just that day, Jack's mother had told the boy's five-year-old sister, Stephanie, that she didn't think Jack would be coming home but that he would be going to be with God in heaven.

Stephanie's reply to her grieving mommy was this: "Oh! Then he'll get to be with Great Grandma." And, "God has a big backyard, Mommy, and a big house with lots of room!"

Upon returning home, Pastor Matt wrote his first song. In obedience to the Holy Spirit, a man who knew nothing about lyrics or musical notes wrote a beautiful tribute that brought comfort to the one thousand people who heard it at Jack's funeral. Jack's song is featured at the end of this chapter.

Stay open to the ways the Spirit may want to use you in the lives of people, especially those in a season of pain. He may call you to do something you have never done before. Ask him.

a verse to meditate upon

*Those who sow in tears will reap with songs of joy.
He who goes out weeping, carrying seed to sow,
will return with songs of joy.*

PSALM 126:5-6

"God's Big Backyard"
(Jack's song)

BY MATT STEMME AND CHRIS VAN DUYN[5]

God has a house with many rooms
And a place He prepared for me
There's all kinds of toys, for girls and for boys
And a swing set that you should see

Refrain:

All of this and more
In God's big backyard (repeat)

Jesus is here
He knows my name
He greets me with hugs and kisses
Laughing and singin' and playin' baseball
I never miss when He pitches

Repeat refrain.

Great Grandma and me sitting under a tree
Readin' all of my favorite stories

We sing "Shout to the Lord" just as loud as we can
And chase all the little puppies

Repeat refrain.

You know, I heard ya praying
Thanks for hearin' what I'm sayin'
Jesus is here with me playin'
In God's big backyard

Now, Mommy, don't you worry
Hey, Dad, I'm not too far
Remember, I'm just playin'
In God's big backyard

One day we all will be playing
In God's big backyard

prayers *that* start *when the* enemy prowls

The enemy can't take away my salvation, but he can try to keep me in places of bondage and defeat so that I do not move out in the power and forgiveness that is rightfully mine by way of the Cross. His tactics have shown up most often for me in my role as a mother.

As soon as the banana bread slipped from his hands and headed toward the ground, my

son looked up at me. I spontaneously reacted by rolling my eyes and giving him a look of frustration, which I immediately regretted even before the look on his face fell. I approached him, cupped his face in my hands, and said, "It's okay, Buddy. It was slippery, and everybody makes mistakes," yet even as I spoke the words I knew that it was too late—the damage was done. My facial expression had given away my heart's true feelings. After I dropped my son off at school, I drove home feeling guilty and sad.

On my knees at home, I cried out to God, confessing this behavior that regularly hurts my children. I prayed for God to change me. I prayed that he would stop my facial expressions before they start, and that he would give me more grace for my children. As I prayed and cried, I sensed God's presence. It was as if he said to me, "Even now, my child, with this mistake that you have made, I do not look at you with condemnation but with love. Take this in, look at my face, for this is what will change you...my grace. As you

allow yourself to receive this grace deeply, you will be able to extend it to your children."

I realized in that moment that while Spencer had dropped the banana bread, I had dropped Spencer. Yet when I looked at my heavenly Father, his eyes were not filled with frustration and exasperation, but with grace and compassion.

His grace moves me out of the prison the enemy wants to keep me locked up in. Jesus is the key to freedom from guilt, shame, and all other false accusations.

scriptural prayer

Lord, please help me to remember that my struggle is not against flesh and blood, but against the rulers, against the authorities, against the powers of this dark world, and against the spiritual forces of evil in the heavenly realms. In knowing this, Lord, teach me how to be strong in you and in your mighty power. (Based on Ephesians 6:10, 12)

accidents *and* grace

Let the accidents and incidents of this day drive you to your knees and to the throne of grace. The enemy wants you to feel "bad" and he wants you to feel "shame," but God wants you to know you are loved and forgiven. Have you failed someone today? Pour out your feelings to the One who knows you best and loves you the most.

keep *a* short list

Even with lessons learned and tools in hand, there are times I still choose my way instead of God's way. This is called sin, and one of its consequences is that it can "give the devil a foothold" (Ephesians 4:27). Coming to God on a regular basis and asking him to examine my heart and to light up the dark places gives me an opportunity to stay in constant relationship with him. Ask God to examine your heart today.

a fresh outpouring

The Bible teaches in Galatians 5:16 that if you "live by the Spirit...you will not gratify the desires of the sinful nature." With this in mind, remember to ask for a fresh outpouring of the Holy Spirit following times of repentance so that you might steer clear of the paths where the enemy prowls.

shift your focus

Ask God to show you clearly what he thinks of prayer and the priority that he places on it. Fern Nichols, the founder of Moms In Touch International, says, "I believe that Satan has us thinking that being spiritual means being productive. He doesn't want us to cross over the invisible line into powerful intercessory prayer. If he can keep us thinking that being on the productive side of the line is doing great things for God, then we will secure few blessings for our family, schools, community and nation."[2]

our enemy is a...

liar and a murderer (JOHN 8:44)

deceiver and accuser (REVELATION 12:9–10)

tempter (MATTHEW 4:3)

Take some time to really look at this list. These are just some of the names the enemy is given in Scripture. Ask God to help you become more aware and alert to the ways the enemy "shows his face" in your life.

"beauty *and the* beast"

By reading the outstanding new book *Captivating*, I learned something relevant about the enemy. When speaking of Lucifer before his fall, Ezekiel 28:12 tells us, "'You were the model of perfection, full of wisdom and perfect in beauty.'" Authors John and Stasi Eldredge explain, "Satan fell because of his beauty. Now his heart for revenge is to assault beauty...she [woman] allures the world to God. He hates it with a jealousy we can only imagine."[3] Knowing that one of the ways I will be assaulted is in the area of beauty has increased my ability to pray specifically and fight back with the truth. Do the same today.

fierce protection

Get an "Oh, no you don't" attitude with the enemy. When you are tempted to choose your way, realize who may be at work there. Prayer is powerful, and the enemy will use many tactics to keep you from accessing that power. Time and again I have seen moms with the best intentions of joining our Moms In Touch prayer meeting finding that "something came up." When something comes up in your life, get on your knees with even more gumption, even if it means rescheduling that something for another time of the day.

> *All hell cannot tear a boy or girl away*
> *from a praying mother.*
> —BILLY SUNDAY[4]

get dressed

As you put on your clothes today, verbally put on the "full armor of God." Write out the following Scripture verse and place it in your closet or on your bathroom mirror so that you always remember to "get dressed" first thing in the morning.

Put on the full armor of God so that you can take your stand against the devil's schemes.... Stand firm then, with the belt of truth buckled around your waist, with the breastplate of righteousness in place, and with your feet fitted with the readiness that comes from the gospel of peace. In addition to all this, take up the shield of faith, with which you can extinguish all the flaming arrows of the evil one. Take the helmet of salvation and the sword of the Spirit, which is the word of God.

EPHESIANS 6:11; 14–17

turn up *the* volume

Turn on your stereo and get the praise music on wherever you are. As often as you can, keep it on and sing along. Speaker/author Thelma Wells uses this technique, explaining that "Satan and the Lord cannot occupy the same territory (place). Keep your praise music on."

lion eyes

When my children started school, I felt called to begin a prayer group for the students and the school. I met with a woman who had led groups like this for years. The first thing she told me was: "Beware of the spirit of discouragement. It is the enemy's tool to keep you off of your knees." I appreciated the advance warning of what form the enemy might come in. Pray that your eyes would be enlightened to the enemy so that in the power of the Spirit you can "Resist him, standing firm in the faith."

power out *the* praise

If you sense any form of evil, declare praises in the form of Scripture verses or songs. You can also speak the name of the Lord out loud and "stand firm in the faith." (See chapter 2 for descriptions of the names of God.)

don't take it in

Psalm 119:37 reads: "Turn my eyes away from worthless things." Pray today for the Lord to show you if there is anything your eyes are taking in that he considers worthless (magazines, books, movies). Pray that God would give you the strength to "turn away."

open your mouth wide

Participate in the beautiful act of Communion as often as possible. This is a reminder of the sacrifice Jesus made for you personally. In humble gratitude come to the table that God has prepared for you and take in all that he has for you. When you leave the table and go out into the world, declare verbally, "The one who is in [me] is greater than the one who is in the world" (1 John 4:4).

keep it *in the* light

James 5:16 says, "Confess your sins to each other and pray for each other so that you may be healed." Are you a part of a fellowship of believers? If not, pray that the Lord would guide you to such a fellowship. If you are already connected, ask the Lord if there is an area in your life in which he wants you to experience healing through confession to the body of Christ. "As long as we do not admit that the deep things of our heart are there ... these rooms of our heart become darkened and the enemy sets up shop there to accuse us."[5]

falsely accused

Do you often feel the need to defend yourself to others? Have you been hurt by gossip or slander? Take a minute and read Psalm 109:1–4. The psalmist seems to be suffering from similar attacks, yet we read in verse 4: "But I give myself to prayer" (NKJV). Today instead of opening your mouth to defend yourself, invest that energy into prayer and praise (see vv. 30–31). Let your God defend you today.

talk back

The enemy is a liar and a deceiver, and when he is at work, you need to talk back to him with the power of God's truth. What are the lies the enemy is whispering in your ear today? Speak God's Word back to him today and watch him flee.

stay *in the* game

"March madness" is just that in our home. I've noticed that when a team makes a basket, they celebrate exuberantly, but just as quickly they get back to their defensive positions. My husband has informed me that this is called "transitioning." The team members have learned that if they focus on their victory for too long, they will quickly lose ground. When you have experienced victory, pray for eyes that are alert to the enemy positioned for battle. The enemy would like nothing more than to bring you down when you least expect it.

stay out of reach

A few years ago my children were involved in a scary situation, the details of which had been kept from me. I "very energetically" told my husband how things should have been done differently. The Lord soon made me aware that I was going to a place of pride when what I was really feeling was fear. Jonathan Edwards said, "Nothing sets a person so much out of the devil's reach as humility."[6] Pray for humility, asking the Lord to show you if there are any areas of pride in your life. The pride might be hiding a feeling that you have mistakenly labeled "weakness."

ask the right question

When facing decisions today, ask yourself this question: "Does this have the potential to overpower me and ultimately master me?" God's Word teaches, "'Everything is permissible for me'—but I will not be mastered by anything" (1 Corinthians 6:12). With a prayerful attitude, this question can help you to keep Jesus as your one and only Master.

exit stage left

When you feel tempted, ask God to show you the way out. When he shows you what it is, pray for the grace and strength to follow through and obey immediately. Read 1 Corinthians 10:13 to learn more about this promise.

catch *the* lies

Write down the negative words and sentences that consistently roll around in your head. For years I thought I had low self-esteem, but the more aware I became of God's truth, the more I realized that my negative self-talk was actually the enemy at work. Some of the "lies" that I wrote down included: "Who do you think you are?" "Nobody will help you; nobody cares about what you need." "You are on your own, so you better figure it out for yourself."

replace *the* lie with truth

Using a red pen, write: "The Truth" from God's Word next to the sentences that you wrote down under "Catch the Lies." For example, next to "Who do you think you are?" I wrote, "I am a child of God" (1 John 3:1). Keep this list close at hand—in your purse, next to your bed, or in a drawer in the kitchen. Verbally declare the truth in those times that the "tape" of the enemy starts playing in your head.

get out

As a believer, you have been given authority to rebuke the enemy. This day, demand verbally that any power of darkness flee in the name of Jesus. Walk through your home, proclaiming that this territory is covered with the blood of the Lamb and that because of that the forces of evil must leave. Pray that the Lord would cancel any plan the enemy might have for you or your family. Tell the enemy to "Get out!"

> *"I have given you authority to trample on snakes and scorpions and to overcome all the power of the enemy; nothing will harm you."*
>
> **LUKE 10:19**

stay balanced

Being aware of the battle and being obsessed with the battle are two very different things. Be alert to the enemy, *but* remain fixed on Christ. When we focus on anything (a problem, a fear, our finances, a relationship, the enemy) too intently, everything else can fade away. Pray today that Jesus Christ would be at the center of your focus and that he would develop in you a healthy balance for the battle at hand.

> *My eyes are ever on the LORD, for only he will release my feet from the snare.*
>
> **PSALM 25:15**

tent of protection

Pray today for a tent of protection around your home, your heart, and the loved ones in your life. Pray for a spirit of unity in your marriage and in your relationships. If you have "opened any door for the enemy," pray that the Lord would shut it. Thank the Lord today for his promise: "No weapon turned against you will succeed" (Isaiah 54:17 NLT).

safeguard future generations

In the Bible we are taught that the sins of the fathers reach to the third and fourth generation (see Exodus 20:5–6). Our choices (good and bad) not only affect us but also future generations. Take a good look at your family history and decide in prayer what territory you will take back from the enemy by saying no to sin. Commit in prayer to leaving a legacy of love.

If you are feeling the need to understand more about the topic of spiritual warfare or you are feeling that there are areas of bondage in your life, make this a matter of prayer and consider investing in an in-depth study, such as Beth Moore's *Breaking Free*[7] or Neil T. Anderson's *Victory Over the Darkness*.[8]

a verse to meditate upon

"The thief comes only to steal and kill and destroy; I have come that they may have life, and have it to the full."

JOHN 10:10

kissing *the* foot *of the* cross

Where the Father hung my sins
Were it not for this one act of love
I would stand condemned

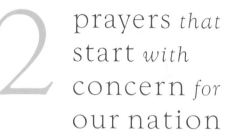

12 prayers *that* start *with* concern *for* our nation

She was only sixteen years old when she rode her horse on that dark and stormy night in 1777. Through wooded and dangerous territory she galloped, stopping at isolated farmhouses. Rapping on the door with a stick, she would cry out, "The British are burning Danbury! Muster at Ludingtons'!"[2]

By the end of her forty-mile trek, young Sybil Ludington had "called to arms" the militia that was under her father's command. Her brave actions enabled the soldiers to gather quickly, and ultimately resulted in the British being turned back. Sybil's bold act of courage was instrumental in the very foundation of the freedom that we live with today in America.

There is a statue of Sybil in Carmel, New York, on the path of her "midnight ride." It is a huge bronze rendering of her on horseback, arm raised, stick in hand, calling out her message. The statue stands as a reminder to all that a nation was affected by one young girl's act of bravery.

I learned as an adult that this Revolutionary War heroine is one of my ancestors, and I was immediately inspired by this girl called "The Female Paul Revere." I felt a renewed passion to ride with courage through the darkness of society and sound the alarm to mothers, exhorting them to take back the power that they have to affect this country by harnessing God's power through prayer. I felt inspired to tell women that we all need to

be like Sybil and do our part to hold back that which would seek to overtake and destroy. But then some questions came up for me: How did the Ludingtons raise a daughter of such character? A child that so willingly stepped forward when she was needed? What occurred in her home that caused courage to grow?

These questions brought me to the conclusion that the true "Sybils" in our lives are the children in our midst.

I have not seen a record of Mrs. Ludington's mothering techniques, nor do I even know if they were a churchgoing family. But I do know that 2 Chronicles 20:15 states: "The battle is not yours, but God's."

If we as mothers are to send our children out into the world to affect it, to change it, to bring revival, we must commit to "take up [our] positions" (2 Chronicles 20:17) and seek God. Indeed, in order to accomplish the lofty goal of changing a nation, we must prepare and equip through prayer, one child at a time. As the story of Sybil Ludington shows, even a child has the power to change the course of history.

scriptural prayer

"We will not hide them from their children; we will tell the next generation the praiseworthy deeds of the LORD, his power, and the wonders he has done. He decreed statutes for Jacob and established the law in Israel, which he commanded our forefathers to teach their children, so the next generation would know them, even the children yet to be born, and they in turn would tell their children" (Psalm 78:4–6).

reflection

I attended a funeral a few years back for a friend's mother.[3] At that funeral I was struck by how each of her children recalled the same scene: their widowed, weary, and working mother kneeling at the foot of her bed in prayer. Pray that you would be a mother who would seek Jesus on behalf of her children no matter how weary you may be.

look it up

Open your Bible today to Deuteronomy 6:4–9.
As you read these verses, ask the Holy Spirit to
guide and direct your thoughts. Pray for specific
ideas that you can employ to make loving God
and telling your children about him a reality in
your home. When you receive an idea, write it
down and put it into practice.

the right place *at the* right time

I have heard many mothers cry about their failures with their children. When you feel this
way, remember that the Lord hand-selected you
to raise your children; it was no accident.
Turn to Acts 17:26–27 and ask God
to give your mother's heart
encouragement and peace.

my kid has character!

A girlfriend gave me a bookmark that I use every day. Compiled by Bob Hostetler, it lists thirty-one biblical virtues to pray about for your children. There is one virtue for each day of the month. I keep it in my Bible where it reminds me to pray daily, scripturally, and specifically for my children. The specific bookmark that I have is available at *www.NavPress.com* in conjunction with their periodical *Pray!* Consider using one to pray for your children.

program prayers

Church programs are a great opportunity for your children to grow in their knowledge and love of Jesus (hopefully planting the seeds of godly character). Whether they are in Sunday school, youth group, or vacation Bible school, they are sure to be praying, learning, and fellowshiping. Pray and ask God where you should take your children to participate, and then pray that your kids would enjoy it.

Bible traditions

Purchase an age-appropriate Bible for you and your children to read together. Create your own Bible traditions, whether it is a bedtime reading or turning to the Word in times of challenges and difficulties. Pray that a love for the Word would grow in your children.

what do I do?

In any given situation, seek the Lord. Whether you are trying to decide what school to send your child to, or you need to know what the proper discipline would be for the circumstance at hand, or you are simply at a loss. Go to the Source of all wisdom.

Trust in the LORD with all your heart and lean not on your own understanding; in all your ways acknowledge him, and he will make your paths straight.

PROVERBS 3:5-6

a woman's touch

I remember my mother's prayers and they have always followed me. They have clung to me all my life.

—ABRAHAM LINCOLN[4]

Whose prayers have "clung" to you? Who prayed for you and your character development? Was it your grandma? A neighbor? Your best friend's parents? As you remember this person, say a prayer of blessing and thanksgiving for them.

have *an* effect

In 2 Timothy 1:5 the apostle Paul acknowledges to young Timothy that his faith was greatly impacted by the women in his life, specifically his grandmother and his mother. If you are a single mother or you are the spiritual leader in your home, be encouraged by this passage.

Look it up and meditate on it. Thank God today for the opportunity to affect the children in your life through the power of the Holy Spirit.

fan *the* flame

My daughter has always had an amazing memory. I often tell her what a wonderful gift the Lord has given her in this and that he is going to use it in a mighty way. Ask the Lord to show you the gifts that he has placed in the children in your life and then affirm them verbally. Pray that they would use their gifts for his glory.

baptize *the* nations

My girlfriend's two children decided that they were ready to be baptized. She invited our family to the event. Before attending, our children asked many questions about baptism, leading us to pray and search the Scriptures together. By the time the day arrived there were seven children ready to be baptized. Attend events such as baptisms together as a family, and prayerfully answer questions as they arise. Pray that your children would one day...

> ...go and make disciples of all nations, baptizing them in the name of the Father and of the Son and of the Holy Spirit, and teaching them to obey everything I have commanded you.
>
> **MATTHEW 28:19-20**

hope *for the* future

What are your hopes for future generations? What are your dreams for your grandchildren and great-grandchildren? I wrote this in my journal one year ago:

> *My dream for my grandchildren is that they would be worshipers of the King of Kings, full of God's grace and truth, winning the hearts of the world to the Good News of Jesus Christ.*

Take a few minutes to write down your "hope for the future." Keep your "hope" close at hand to remind you to pray that it would become a reality.

pray *the* roster

Your realm of influence is often larger than your own home. One way that I remember to pray for the other children in my life is to pray down the roster of my children's sports teams or to pray through a class picture. Take a few minutes today to pray for all the children in your life. Pray that they would come to a saving knowledge of Jesus Christ and that they would affect this country in a positive way.

dinner dialogue

Take a few minutes during the dinner hour to explain to your children the importance of praying for our country and then pray and sing a few patriotic songs together.

Blessed is the nation whose God is the LORD.
PSALM 33:12

mark your calendars

The first Thursday in May is the National Day of Prayer. Join with thousands by praying for our nation on that day. You can do this in the privacy of your home or at your church or school. See the Web site *www.nationaldayofprayer.org* for ideas and articles, including a great resource called "Freedom Five."

flag *a* prayer

Ask your children to be on the lookout for the "stars and stripes." When they point out an American flag, agree in prayer for our troops. Pray that the soldiers would be protected, that their eyes would be open to danger, and that they would seek the Lord during this time of combat.

pledge allegiance

As you stand to recite these familiar words, pray that your nation would always be "one nation under God." Teach your children to pray for a spirit of unity to grow among the citizens of this country and for many to become worshipers of the King of Kings and Lord of Lords.

cast your vote

At election times explain to your children the privilege and value of voting. Take the time to pray for discernment before casting your personal vote, and pray that in all of your actions you will be a godly example to your children.

presidential prayer team

Check out this great Web site: *www.presidential prayerteam.com*. You can find specific prayer requests for the president and other leaders here. There is even a kids' link that is full of interesting facts, colorful pictures, and great prayer ideas for children. Then sit down and pray with your kids for our president.

Memorial Day prayers

A park just opened in our town to honor those who serve our country (past and present) through the military. It is a lovely place with flags representing each military division, bricks with the names of loved ones who have served, fountains, green grass, and benches. It is a great place to bring children to educate them and to pray with them. Take your kids to a museum or a memorial and guide them in prayer for our nation.

parade prayers

Take the opportunity to bring your kids to your local Fourth of July parade or to watch a parade on television. When you see the military represented, take the opportunity to tell your children about it and pray with them for those in the military.

map it out

Get your children place mats imprinted with the United States of America as a mealtime reminder to pray for the nation, one state at a time. Or post a map on the wall next to their beds. Pray for hearts that would come to know Jesus and be transformed.[5]

If my people, who are called by my name, will humble themselves and pray and seek my face and turn from their wicked ways, then will I hear from heaven and will forgive their sin and will heal their land.

2 CHRONICLES 7:14

put feet *to* prayers

Do you know any soldiers or other military personnel? Any wives of military men who are serving away from home? Pray for a specific way that you and your family can serve the family of a person in the military. Get your children involved in the process.

firecrackers

Our family tradition for the Fourth of July is to barbeque with friends and sit out under the evening sky and watch the fireworks. Let this year's show move you and your family to a place of awe for our Lord. Take a few minutes during the show to say a prayer of gratitude to our sovereign God, who has made your home a land of freedom.

The spectacle of a nation praying is more awe-inspiring than the explosion of an atomic bomb. The force of prayer is greater than any possible combination of man-controlled powers, because prayer is man's greatest means of tapping the infinite resources of God.

— J. EDGAR HOOVER [6]

presidential prayers

Whether we are Democrat, Republican, or Independent, we are called to pray for those in places of leadership. (See 1 Timothy 2:1–4.) Each time you see or hear the president (in the media for most of us), say a short prayer for him and his leadership of our country. Ask the Lord to grow in you an increasing respect for this shepherd.

To get nations back on their feet,
we must get down on our knees first.[7]

in *the* news

I am protective of what my children take in when it comes to the news. It seems that every time I turn on the television, I am barraged with kidnappings, rapes, and other unspeakable violence. While it may be necessary to be selective in letting young ones know about current events, there are needs in the news that can lead to healthy conversation and powerful times of prayer as a family. As your heart feels led, share with your children the concerns from the news that offer opportunities to agree in prayer.

committed

Pray for revival in the heart of this nation. Pray that your children would be a part of bringing that revival to pass. Pray that your children would have hearts that are committed to the Lord, committed to prayer, and committed to our nation.

working hands

Whether folded together in prayer or busy folding towels, a mother's hands are always working. As you work at raising boys and girls of virtue and courage, pray that the Lord would do as he promises in Psalm 90:17 and establish the work of your hands.

"sure thing"

My husband and I were preparing for a trip to Europe, which motivated us to meet with our lawyer and get our will in order. As I sat there filling out paper work and answering questions about 401(k)s and IRAs, I became aware of the lack of financial contribution that I make to our family. I felt myself begin to "sink" emotionally as I began to ask myself the question, "What contribution am I making to our family?" The answer came as quickly as the question: "Prayer." Praying for your children is like taking a huge chunk of money and investing it into a "sure thing" on the stock market. It is the personal investment that guarantees the nation and the world the biggest return. Make that investment today by praying for your children.

a verse to
meditate upon

*Sons are a heritage from the LORD, children
a reward from him. Like arrows in the hands
of a warrior are sons born in one's youth.
Blessed is the man whose quiver is full of
them. They will not be put to shame when
they contend with their enemies in the gate.*

PSALM 127:3-5

"*a future not our own*"

BY ARCHBISHOP OSCAR ROMERO[8]

It helps, now and then, to step back and take the long view.
The kingdom is not only beyond our efforts,
it is beyond our vision.
We accomplish in our lifetime only a tiny fraction
of the magnificent enterprise that is God's work.
Nothing we do is complete, which is another way of saying
that the kingdom always lies beyond us.
No statement says all that could be said.
No prayer fully expresses our faith.
No confession brings perfection.
No pastoral visit brings wholeness.
No program accomplishes the church's mission.
No set of goals and objectives includes everything.
This is what we are about.
We plant the seeds that one day will grow.
We water seeds already planted,
knowing they hold future promise.

We lay foundations that will need further development.
We provide yeast that produces effects beyond our capabilities.
We cannot do everything,
and there is a sense of liberation in realizing that.
This enables us to do something, and to do it very well.
It may be incomplete, but it is a beginning,
a step along the way, an opportunity for God's grace
to enter and do the rest.
We may never see the end results,
but that is the difference between the master builder
and the worker.
We are workers, not master builders, ministers, not messiahs.
We are prophets of a future not our own.

starting *and* finishing well:
becoming *a* woman *of* prayer

> *Lord, I want to be free of the pressure to do great things in the world by being great in doing small things for Thee.*
> —**MARIAN WRIGHT EDELMAN**[1]

For months my daughter and I had a little ritual we would partake in after my quiet time was over. She would peek into the living room, and when I was finished praying, I would signal for her to come over. She would climb up into my lap, and we would snuggle for a little while before starting the day.

One morning she looked up at me and held my gaze for several minutes. A playful smile danced around the corners of her mouth and she said, "Mommy, I can see myself in your eyes."

Holding her there, I recalled the grandiose ideas that had entered my mind soon after receiving Christ. I had felt such gratitude for his grace that I felt compelled to do big things for God. I began to dream of changing the world for Christ. I began praying that the Lord would give me opportunities to do these huge spiritual acts of service for him—but to no avail. My standard routine of changing diapers, doing the dishes, and taking the kids to doctors' appointments still existed. It was when I heard speaker Patsy Clairmont[2] talk about a similar situation in her own life that I sat up and took notes.

Patsy, a self-proclaimed agoraphobic (fear of open spaces), had also prayed that the Lord would show her the "big spiritual things" she could do for him. But when she prayed, the answer she got more than once was, "Make the bed!" She went on to explain to the audience that in Scripture we are taught that if we are faithful in the little things (like making the bed), more will be added unto us.

It dawned on me that I was not even being faithful in the "little things," such as having a daily time of prayer with Jesus or having a good attitude while serving the Lord in my own home. Yet I was asking for greater responsibilities. I began taking God at his word that day by being faithful with my part and waiting on his timing for the bigger things.

Now I sat literally holding Grace on my lap. A few years of being faithful in the little things had indeed blessed me with big things, like this sacred moment with my daughter.

scriptural prayer

Lord, it is my desire to seek first your kingdom and your righteousness, and to trust you when you say that all these things will be given to me as well. Please show me how I can accomplish this in my life. (Based on Matthew 6:33)

quiet time

My life truly changed when I began participating in a daily structured time of prayer, often called a "quiet time." I do not believe that I would be able to "pray without ceasing" had I not ceased from playing and doing long enough to sit quietly at the feet of my Lord in the first place. Pray about making a commitment to a daily set-apart quiet time.

> *Prayer must not be our chance work, but our daily business, our habit and vocation.... We must addict ourselves to prayer.*
> —CHARLES SPURGEON[3]

a tisket, *a* tasket

Fill a basket with all the things you will need for your quiet time: a Bible, a journal, pens and highlighters, tissue, stationery and stamps, devotional or study material, a candle and matches. Place your basketful of blessings near your favorite quiet time location and pray that your heart would be "filled" with the power of Christ every time you reach into it.

nesting

When I decided to have a regular quiet time, I wanted to look forward to it. I chose a location in my home that was well lit. I placed a warm blanket on the chair and a scented candle on the nearby table, and I made myself a steaming cup of tea. Ask God to show you what would motivate you to meet with him daily.

timing is everything

Pray that the Lord would help you make this time with him. Are you a morning or a night person? If you are a planner, get your calendar out and pencil it in. If you think that starting out with a Monday through Friday schedule might be more realistic for you than a daily one, do that. Follow the advice of Becky Tirabassi and "Make an appointment with the King and keep it!"[4]

rally *the* troops

Ask for support. If you are going to have a morning quiet time, inevitably the kids will choose to get up thirty minutes earlier that day. Ask your husband or someone else for help with tending the kids for that window of time. When my kids were little, I started my quiet time at six in the morning. The night before, I put their sippy cups in the fridge so that if they woke up early, my husband could simply give them their cups and turn on *Sesame Street*.

on guard

Do not be surprised by resistance and opposition as you commit yourself to prayer. Pray about this.

Lord, please protect this time with you. I know that the enemy does not want me to be on my knees, because that is where battle is done and changes occur. Give me the eyes to see when "distractions" are not innocent but diversions from my time with you. Fix my eyes on you and guard our time together, Lord.

seasons of prayer

For the first two years of prayer, I enjoyed an afternoon quiet time, but as the children got older their naps got shorter and my quiet time was no longer "quiet." I began to ask the Lord when I should pray, all the while informing him that I am not a morning person. You guessed it, he called me to get up *early*. I relented, trusting that if he was calling me to get up early, he was going to provide the energy necessary to get me through the rest of the day. Stay flexible with your quiet time, and listen to God tell you when he wants to be with you.

prayer expedition

Pray about doing a "quiet-time trade" with a girlfriend. Doing an extended quiet time *away* from the house once a week may be more realistic for you than a daily quiet time. Ask a girlfriend if you can swap baby-sitting with her on a regular basis. One good rule of thumb is to go somewhere free of distractions. For some that may be a coffee shop or a park; for others it may be in your home.[5]

stealing quiet time

Keep a quiet-time bag/basket in the car. You just might be able to steal some time here and there while you wait at the doctor's office or in the school pickup line. Ask God to show you ways to find time for him.

playland prayer

Take your quiet-time bag/basket to a playland/playground or park. When the kids run off and play, open up your heart to the Lord. While it may not be a "quiet" time, it may very well be an uninterrupted time of fellowship with Christ.

fresh start

I have experienced extended periods in my prayer time when for one reason or another (getting sick, going on vacation) I missed a day, and then another. If this occurs for you, instead of beating yourself up or throwing your hands in the air, turn back to God, confessing that you've missed him.

expectation

Psalm 5:3 reads, "In the morning, O LORD, you hear my voice; in the morning I lay my requests before you and wait in expectation." After you have laid your requests before the Lord through your quiet time, ask God to keep your eyes open throughout the day in expectation of seeing him at work in your life.

the invitation

One of my friends has a terrific prayer idea. She leaves her Bible open on the dining room table as an invitation. When she can "steal away" for a few minutes, her quiet time is waiting for her. Is there a place where you can leave yourself an invitation? Look around your house and see if there is a corner for you.

prayer traditions

When you are on vacation or experiencing a unique schedule (Easter break with the kids), get creative with your quiet time. Our family goes to a cabin for a week each summer. Over the years Grace and I have developed a prayer tradition for this time of the year. I take my tea, Bible, and journal onto the porch overlooking the lake. When Grace wakes up, she meets me with her blanket. We sit together looking out on the lake, singing praise songs and reading Scripture together. It is a very special prayer tradition.

come boldly

Think for a moment about what a privilege it is that we get to converse face-to-face with God. When Jesus died on the cross, the temple curtain (that kept God hidden) was torn in two, allowing access to the inner courts of dialogue with God Most High (through Jesus). Wow! Pray that the Lord would grow a sense of wonder in you regarding this awesome privilege and then come boldly to the throne on a regular basis.

shut *the* door

In Matthew 6:5–6 Jesus tells us not to pray "standing...on the street corners," but rather to "go into your room, close the door and pray to your Father, who is unseen." There are times when our prayers are to be hidden from the world, maybe so we aren't focusing on "looking spiritual." Today go into a room, close the door, and quiet yourself before the Lord. You can retreat to a small closet or even a bathroom with a lock. There need only be room enough for you and your Father and time enough to say, "I love you and I need you."

discipline *and* desire

In those first few weeks of having a regular quiet time, I experienced "discomfort" in many ways. Getting up early was not fun, figuring out what to pray about felt contrived, and questions like, "Is this really going to change anything?" nagged at me. At some point during those set-aside times, God moved me out of my discomfort and into his presence. This happened regularly enough that the act that began as a discipline quickly moved into something desirable. Pray that your discipline would be blessed by becoming a heartfelt longing and a thirsting after God.

finishing strong

Getting up early and praying is now a part of my routine, just as much as brushing my teeth. Lately I've noticed that while my days have been starting out great, they have not been finishing as well. I am in the process of creating some new evening habits, because the channel surfing and kitchen grazing are doing me in. Ask God to show you one small action you can take this evening that would help you to "finish strong." It may be reflecting on the Scriptures from earlier in the day or uttering a short prayer of thanksgiving for another day full of grace.

up *to the* mountain

I am a huge advocate of retreats. There is something signifi-
cant in saying, "I am choosing to turn away from the life
that is screaming for my attention and to turn toward God,
trusting that he will meet me." Pray about going on a
retreat. It may be a church retreat, a silent retreat, or a time
when you choose, for instance, to go to your in-laws' vacation
home for a day to be alone with the Lover of your soul.

doing battle

If you were fighting in a war, would you leave your home
without taking into consideration what was waiting for
you on the outside? Wouldn't you anticipate the attacks
that might come your way and prepare accordingly? Today
make your prayer time a time of preparation for the
battle, a time that you are using to fight for
those you love. "Living on the offensive in prayer with God prevents
having to be on the defensive in
war with the devil."[6]

accountability

Enlist the help of a friend or family member to ask you on occasion, "How's your quiet time going?" Or perhaps that person could ask you what you are learning from the Lord these days, assuming that you are being consistent with your prayer time. This is not about being legalistic, but about being held accountable and being encouraged to turn to God. I got a card a few years ago from a friend that was signed, "A true friend is one who turns you toward God." These are the kinds of friends that we all need.

carpe diem

The first talk I ever gave was entitled "Seize the Day!" It came about as a result of my first year in prayer. When I began to "seek first the kingdom," instead of worrying about all the things that needed to be done, the Lord brought many blessings into my life, including a speaking ministry. Read Luke 12:22–34 today and exchange your worry for worship through a time of prayer.

structure

How do you structure your quiet time? Perhaps you currently start in the Word and then move to prayer, but later feel drawn to journal first. The structure may change over months and years. Remain open while at the same time sticking to the essentials of being in the Word and taking the time to pray. Spend some time today asking God to help you develop a prayer routine for this month.

look back

After you have been consistently praying and journaling, spend a few quiet times in prayerful reflection. Look back over your journals or through the notes from a study. Has there been a theme? Can you see areas where the Lord has helped you grow? Do you see ways that he has answered a specific prayer? Try this faith-building exercise during the month of your birthday.

desires *and* dreams

"One day I will be the National Aerobics champion, and I will have an exercise video!" My husband still teases me about the fact that I informed him of this on one of our first dates. This "burning desire" remained in me even after my children were born. As I began to pray consistently, the Lord gave me some of my dreams (I got the chance to be in an exercise video), but he also changed my desires and gave me new dreams. (He took my desire to be an aerobics champion away and gave me a new desire—to serve him through motivational speaking.) Pray, "Lord, I want what you want for me."

Delight yourself in the LORD, and he will give you the desires of your heart.

PSALM 37:4

hide *and* seek

When you find yourself comparing yourself to others, whether their achievements, their children's accomplishments, or their dress size, let it be a reminder for you to stop and pray. Go to your prayer time with the desire to discover what God's plan and purpose is for *your* life. God will begin to reveal it as you seek him. You will not find the answers out in the world because "your life is now hidden with Christ in God" (Colossians 3:2–3).

how do you pray?

Ask people you know, meet, or admire how they spend their quiet time. This is a great way to glean methods and ideas you can try so that you can discover what works best for you during the different seasons of your life. Then try some of these methods, asking God to give you wisdom in the process.

heart position

"Praying without ceasing" isn't about staying in your quiet-time chair with the Bible on your lap 24/7. It is about "an inner, secret turning to God" that "can be made fairly steady, after weeks and months and years of practice, lapses, failures and returns."[7] Give yourself grace for those lapses and failures, confess them to God in prayer, and then return to the practice of a daily quiet time. With this discipline comes an increased awareness of the love and power of Christ, which is available to you unceasingly.

a verse to meditate upon

As the deer pants for streams of water, so my soul pants for you, O God. My soul thirsts for God, for the living God. When can I go and meet with God?

PSALM 42:1-2

"the cry of my heart"

Lord, make me a woman that
Loves you immeasurably
Trusts you unconditionally and
Seeks you wholeheartedly

14

Jesus'
prayer
for us

> *Therefore, since we are receiving a*
> *kingdom that cannot be shaken,*
> *let us be thankful, and so worship*
> *God acceptably with reverence and awe,*
> *for our "God is a consuming fire."*
>
> **HEBREWS 12:28–29**

A few years ago my family gave a surprise birthday party for my grandfather. In an effort to make a memorable gift, we sent out a letter with the invitations, requesting that guests write down a fond memory they had shared with Grandpa or a lesson they had learned by observing him. We then gathered these letters and made an album for Grandpa. To our delight, he loved it.

One of the letters in that album was from my cousin Erik, who was a high school student at the time. Erik wrote about the moment he came to realize the depth of love my grandfather had for him and his sister.

Grandpa was an I-say-jump-you-say-how-high retired lieutenant colonel of the U.S. Army, and many people had never seen the softer side of this wonderful man. My cousin Erik signed his letter to his grandfather, "I wish everyone knew you the way I do."

I believe this to be Jesus' prayer for us. I believe he wants us to know God the Father as he does and to approach Abba as he does. Jesus and his Father were always in close relationship—they were in constant communication with each other. At its core this is what prayer is: being in relationship and constantly communicating with the One you love.

I hope this book has helped you not only to start this type of relationship but that it has also caused your heart to burn with the power and love of Jesus Christ.

May the LORD make you increase,
both you and your children.
May you be blessed by the LORD,
the Maker of heaven and earth.

PSALM 115:14–15

Tracy Klehn is a dynamic speaker, has been a fitness professional for more than sixteen years, and facilitates small groups, Bible studies, and Moms in Touch prayer groups. She, her husband, and their two young children live in Southern California.

endnotes

Introduction

1. John Bunyan, quoted by Leonard Allen, *The Contemporaries Meet the Classics on Prayer* (W. Monroe, LA: Howard Publishing, 2003), 15.

2. Becky Tirabassi, in her talk "Let Prayer Change Your Life" at an Aspiring Women's Conference, Anaheim, CA, February 22, 1998. Used by permission.

3. Richard Foster, *Prayer: Finding the Heart's True Home* (New York: HarperSanFrancisco, 1992), 118.

Chapter 2

1. Edwin Keith, quoted in Frank S. Mead, *12,000 Religious Quotations* (Grand Rapids, MI: Baker Books, 1989), 342.

2. Brennan Manning, adapted from *The Ragamuffin Gospel* (Sisters, OR: Multnomah, 2000), 234. Used by permission.

3. Steven Curtis Chapman, "Let Us Pray" from Signs of Life (Sparrow Records, 1996). Used by permission.

4. Anthony M. Coniaris, "The Jesus Prayer," *Introducing the Orthodox Church* (Minneapolis, MN: Light and Life Publications, 1982), 203-204, 206-207. Used by permission.

5. Kay Arthur, *The Peace and Power of Knowing God's Name* (Colorado Springs: Waterbrook, 2002), 2. Used by permission.

Chapter 3

1. Dolley Carlson, *Gifts From the Heart* (Colorado Springs: Victor Books, 1998), 52.

2. Janet Holm McHenry, *Prayer Walk* (Colorado Springs: Waterbrook, 2002).

3. Thank you, Jenna Klar, for this creative variation on the Christmas card prayer idea.

Chapter 4

1. Ole Hallesby, *Prayer*, trans. Clarence J. Carlsen (Minneapolis, MN: Augsburg, 1959), 141.

2. Based on a sermon by Dr. David White, NorthPark Community Church, December 2004.

3. Fanny Crosby, "Blessed Assurance" (Public domain, 1873), *www.cyberhymnal.com*.

4. Thank you, Maureen Vicaro, for permission to use your words of wisdom in this book!

5. Cece Winans, *Throne Room* (Brentwood, TN: Integrity, 2004), 81-82.

Chapter 5

1. Quoted in Kathleen Norris, *The Cloister Walk* (New York: Riverhead Books, 1996), xxi.

2. Patsy Clairmont speaking on marriage during the question and answer period at the Women of Faith Daytime Intensive in Anaheim, California (September 2002).

3. Becky Tirabassi taught on the topic "Let Prayer Change Your Life" at the Aspiring Women's Conference in Anaheim, California, on February 22, 1998. Used by permission.

4. *Webster's Ninth New Collegiate Dictionary* (Merriam-Webster Inc., 1985).

Chapter 6

1. Becky Tirabassi spoke on the topic "Let Prayer Change Your Life." Used by permission.

2. See *www.awildcanary.com* for more about Father Pat's ministry.

3. Dawson Trotman, quoted in Rick Warren, *The Purpose-Driven Life* (Grand Rapids, MI: Zondervan, 2002), 308.

4. Laurie Beth Jones, *The Path* (New York: Hyperion, 1996).

Chapter 7

1. Richard Foster, *Prayer: Finding the Heart's True Home* (New York: HarperCollins, 1992), 3.

2. Ruth G. Gibson, thank you for your wisdom, your prayers, and your support.

3. John Wooden with Steve Jamison, *Personal Best* (New York: McGraw-Hill, 2004), 2.

4. Based on an idea from a couples' retreat that was led by J. P. and Donna Jones, Orange County, California, July 2002.

5. Marita Littauer, *Praying Wives Club* (Colorado Springs: Cook Communications, 2006).

6. John Eldredge, *Wild at Heart* (Nashville: Thomas Nelson, 2001).

7. Gary Chapman, *The Five Love Languages* (Chicago: Moody Press, 1996).

8. Willard F. Harley, *His Needs, Her Needs* (Grand Rapids, MI: Revell, 2001).

Chapter 8

1. *www.brainyquote.com*

2. *www.foxnews.com*

3. Moms In Touch International Newsletter, Winter 2004, "Terror Cannot Stop Prayer" (Poway, CA).

4. Harry Emerson Fosdick, *The Meaning of Prayer* (New York: Young Men's Christian Association, 1915), 81-83, quoted in *The Contemporary Meet the Classics*, 161-62.

Chapter 9

1. William Blake, quoted in Julia Cameron, *The Artist's Way* (New York: Penguin, 2002), xxii.

2. *www.brainyquote.com/authors/m/mother_teresa*

3. You are an inspiration, Kathy Spencer.

Chapter 10

1. Tommy Walker, "Mourning Into Dancing" (Integrity Music, 1992).

2. George Matheson, quoted in L. B. Cowman, *Streams in the Desert* (Grand Rapids, MI: Zondervan, 1997), 460.

3. Jerry Sittser, *A Grace Disguised* (Grand Rapids, MI: Zondervan, 1995).

4. Hudson Taylor, quoted in *Streams in the Desert*, 188.

5. *Used by permission.*

Chapter 11

1. Samuel Chadwick, quoted in *Nelson's Complete Book of Stories, Illustrations, and Quotes* (Nashville: Thomas Nelson Inc., 2000), 622.

2. Fern Nichols, Moms In Touch International booklet (Poway, CA: Moms In Touch International, 1987), 7.

3. John and Stasi Eldredge, *Captivating* (Nashville: Thomas Nelson, 2005), 84.

4. Quoted in *God's Little Devotional Book for Moms* (Tulsa, OK: Honor Books, 1995), 77.

5. Brent Curtis and John Eldredge, *The Sacred Romance* (Nashville: Thomas Nelson, 1997), 116.

6. Jonathan Edwards, quoted in *The Women of Destiny Bible* (Nashville: Thomas Nelson, 2000), 733.

7. Beth Moore, *Breaking Free* (Nashville: Broadman & Holman, 2000).

8. Neil T. Anderson, *Victory Over the Darkness* (Ventura, CA: Regal, 1997).

Chapter 12

1. Barbara Bush in her commencement address to Wellesley College graduates, 1990, *www.presidentialprayerteam.com.*

2. *www.geocities.com/heartland/plains/1789/sybil.html*;
   Marsha Amstel, *Sybil Ludington's Midnight Ride*
   (Minneapolis: Lerner Publishing Group, 2000).

3. Joel, thank you for allowing me to tell others about your
   godly mother.

4. *www.presidentialprayerteam.com*

5. This idea was adapted from an article by Luis Palau,
   "How to Effectively Proclaim God's Word," *Current
   Thoughts and Trends*, Trendscope Column (October 2002),
   www.navpress.com/magazines/ctt/.

6. Quoted in Frank S. Mead, *12,000 Religious Quotations*, 341.

7. Letter to the Editor, *Des Moines Register*, quoted in *12,000
   Religious Quotations*, 339.

8. *www.archbishoposcarromero.ecsd.net/romero/prayer.html*

Chapter 13

1. Marian Wright Edelman, *Guide My Feet* (New York:
   HarperCollins, 1995), 66.

2. Patsy Clairmont is an author and was a speaker for the
   Women of Faith Conference in Anaheim, California,
   September 1998.

3. Charles Spurgeon, *The Treasures of Charles Spurgeon*
   (Uhrichsville, OH: Barbour, 2004), 64.

4. Becky Tirabassi, from her talk "Let Prayer Change Your
   Life" at the Aspiring Women Conference, Anaheim,
   California, February 1998. Used by permission.
   www.changeyourlifedaily.com

5. Adapted from an idea from Marty Russell at the NorthPark
   Community Church women's retreat.

6. Jill Griffith, *Women of Destiny Bible* (Nashville: Thomas
   Nelson, 2000), 1543.

7. Thomas R. Kelly, quoted in *The Contemporaries Meet the
   Classics on Prayer*, 109.